JUNG'S THOUGHTS ON GOD

On The Hudson
Jung
BOOK SERIES

The Jung on the Hudson Book Series was instituted by the New York Center for Jungian Studies in 1997. This ongoing series is designed to present books that will be of interest to individuals of all fields, as well as mental health professionals, who are interested in exploring the relevance of the psychology and ideas of C. G. Jung to their personal lives and professional activities.

For more information about this series and the New York Center for Jungian Studies contact: Aryeh Maidenbaum, Ph.D., New York Center for Jungian Studies, 41 Park Avenue, Suite 1D, New York, NY 10016, telephone (212) 689-8238, fax (212) 889-7634.

For more information about becoming part of this series contact: Betty Lundsted, Nicolas-Hays, P. O. Box 2039, York Beach, ME 03910-2039, telephone (207) 363-4393 ext. 12, email: nhi@weiserbooks.com.

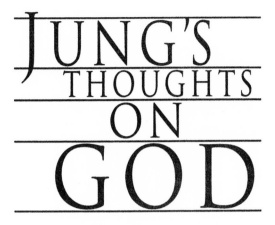

JUNG'S THOUGHTS ON GOD

Religious Depths
of the Psyche

DONALD R. DYER, PH. D.

NICOLAS-HAYS
York Beach, Maine

First published in 2000 by
Nicolas-Hays
P. O. Box 2039
York Beach, ME 03910-2039

Distributed to the trade by
Samuel Weiser, Inc.
P.O. Box 612
York Beach, ME 03910-0612

Copyright © 2000 Donald Dyer

Library of Congress Cataloging-in-Publication Data
Dyer, Donald R.
    Jung's thoughts on God : religious depths of the psyche / Donald R. Dyer.
        p. cm.—Jung on the Hudson book series
    Includes bibliographical references and index.
    ISBN 0-89254-049-4 (alk. paper)
    1. Jung, C. G. (Carl Gustav), 1875–1961—Contributions in doctrine of God. 2. God—History of doctrines—20th century. I. Title. II. Series.
BT98.D94 2000
211'.092—dc21   99–059295

BJ

Cover design by Kathryn Sky-Peck
Typeset in 11/15 Galliard

Printed in United States of America

07 06 05 04 03 02 01 00
8   7   6   5   4   3   2   1

To My Mother
Ethel Mae Jaques Dyer

It is only through the psyche that
we can establish that God acts upon us.

CONTENTS

PREFACE

My acquaintanceship with Jung's story in the later years of my life has brought old concepts of God into new perspective. Realizing that my own thoughts and feelings about God have had some sort of parallel to Jung's experiences in terms of family religious background and early experiences of religion and church has been fascinating. Ideas and experiences of God, which have been fundamental preoccupations in my life since early childhood, reached a high point when I discovered C. G. Jung and his work in 1973, soon after I joined the Religious Society of Friends (commonly known as Quakers). Major impetus came from hearing John R. Yungblut speak, participating in his workshops at Friends General Conference gatherings, and reading his books (*Rediscovering Prayer; Rediscovering the Christ;* and *Discovering God Within*) with his emphasis on the new perspectives of the evolutionary (Teilhard de Chardin) and the depth-psychological (C. G. Jung).

These influences have been expanded by my wife, Marilyn, through her sharing of her voluminous reading of Jung's writings and of books related to Jung's thought, as well as her founding of and dedication to the Jung Society of the Triangle Area (NC) and study groups.

My experiences with the "outer" God through the church and its symbolism have been extensive, starting with my curiosity as a young man in my home town, where I visited all the churches, and continuing into my experiences as a foreign service officer, which included missions to 87 countries, when I worshipped in all the countries of Latin America, as well as in most of the countries of Europe, many in Africa, and a few in Asia. These included Roman Catholic, Eastern Orthodox, Judaic, Muslim, Hindu, and Buddhist worship centers, from which horizons of God-impressions were broadened and deepened by my attempts to assimilate such experiences with my understanding of God.

My life-long interest in God stimulated me to share my understanding of God "out there" and of God "within." I was astounded to discover that Jung used the "God-word" more than *six thousand* times in his writings, and I was determined to organize them in a meaningful way that might help others to examine their own thoughts and feelings and presumptions. Perplexed by polls indicating that an overwhelming proportion of American people say that they believe in God, I would ask them to examine what they really mean by God. Does their "belief" in God result in real meaning in their daily experiences? Does God act? Or, is the greatest value in their lives determined by money, power, sex, family, clan, or something else as the "god" that controls their values and behavior?

—Donald R. Dyer, Ph.D.
Chapel Hill, NC

INTRODUCTION

Carl Gustav Jung has been called an atheist, a modern Gnostic/heretical theologian, and a critical philosopher. Jung viewed himself as an empirical psychologist/scientist, though his suggestions for major changes in Christian theology puzzled his critics so that arguments kept being repeated in a circle of misunderstanding, presumably because Jung viewed such criticisms as part of their agenda but not of his.

Jung paid little attention to God as transcending the universe (out there) and dealt only with immanence (indwelling presence), which tended to become polarized in terms of the metaphysical beliefs of theologians versus Jung's view of the reality of God in the psyche.

One of Jung's fundamental concepts is that, "It is only through the psyche that we can establish that God acts upon us."[1] He goes on to state that there is an archetype of wholeness in the collective unconscious of the psyche which manifests itself spontaneously through dreams, etc., and as such, seems to occupy a central position which "approximates it to the God-image."

Continuing with the idea that we only recognize as real that which acts upon us, Jung assigned to the religious instinct (or need) a human longing for wholeness that

---

[1] C.G. Jung, *Answer to Job* (Princeton, NJ: Princeton University Press, 1973), p. 106.

gathers images of wholeness in the unconscious. These images rise up from the depths of the psychic nature independently of the conscious mind.

Another point of misunderstanding in the criticisms of Jung's writing about God—one that confronts everyone who attempts to write about God—is the limitation of language. In using words about God, one almost inevitably resorts to terms that pose different meanings for different people. As such, Jung himself recognized the common tendency of anthropomorphizing or attributing a human form or personality to God by stating from time to time that, when he uses the word God, he is always referring to the God-image in the psyche, which does not prove the physical existence of God.

Yet, Jung's persistent use of the word "God" in his writings, rather than using the word "God-image," tends to leave open the question of his God-language, so that some readers imagine a metaphysical or real form, such as the common idea of God as an ancient superhuman person sitting on a golden throne somewhere in the cosmos to whom worship is due. Or, as in "olden times," one takes the image of the archetype as the real thing and tries to convert the "imaging" into a physical form without realizing that a symbol is not physical reality, though it is a psychic reality.

An examination of Jung's "God-language" reveals that his use of God-image or image of God (*imago Dei*) occurs only 166 times, and it is concentrated chiefly in writings during the last ten years of his life. Of course, many of his more than 6,000 references to "God" pertain to his extensive writings on the psychology of religion and on alchemy, as in *Answer to Job* (more than 550 references to God and Yahweh), in *Mysterium Coniunctionis: An Inquiry into the Separation and Synthesis of Psychic Opposites in Alchemy* (more than 400), in *Aion: Researches into the Phenomenology of the Self* (more than 300), in *Nietzsche's Zarathustra* (more than 1,000), and in *Psychology and Religion* (more than 200). In many of his writings he is referring to (or quoting from) other author's ideas about God in his analyses and amplifications of the topics, and it is difficult to know if he agrees with a certain writer or not.

Jung said many things about God and used the word more than 300 times in his *Memories, Dreams, Reflections,* which was published in 1962, the year after his death. His conception of religion and spirituality differs in some ways from traditional Christianity, but he explicitly declared his allegiance to Christianity—viewed from the standpoint of psychology and his personal experience of God.

Among the last things he wrote about God was that if we speak of God as an archetype, we are saying nothing about God's real nature, but are letting it be known that God already has a place in that part of our psyche which is pre-existent to consciousness and that therefore God cannot be considered an invention of consciousness. We neither make God more remote, nor eliminate God, but bring God closer to the possibility of being experienced.

It seems that Jung's basic view was that the divine spark or breath of God that lives in the unconscious of human beings can be awakened and can be made conscious so that one may strive for wholeness.

In my attempt to examine the subject of Jung and God, I discovered that there are considerably more than a thousand references to God in the indexes of Jung's works, including *The Collected Works of C. G. Jung, C. G. Jung: Letters, C. G. Jung Speaking,* and *Memories, Dreams, Reflections,* and his seminars. Also daunting is the problem of categorizing God from among the great diversity and controversy of different ideas about God in theology, philosophy, and psychology.

Jung said that people cannot make a conceptual distinction between "God" and "God-image," resulting in an "everlasting contamination of object and image," so that many people think that when one speaks of the "God-image," one is speaking of God and offering "theological" explanations.

As a psychologist, he had to deal with the existence of a God-image in the psyche in much the same way that he reckoned with instinct, but he did not deem himself competent to say what "instinct" really is, it being equally clear to him that the God-image corresponds to a definite complex of psychological facts; but what God really is "remains a question outside the competence of all psychology."[2]

Jung's experiences indicated to him that there is an archetype of wholeness in the depths of the collective unconscious of the psyche/soul that manifests itself in dreams and other energies that strive for consciousness.

---

[2] C. G. Jung, *The Structure and Dynamics of the Psyche* (Princeton, NJ: Princeton University Press, 1969), p. 279.

He interpreted as probable that this archetype is based on the spiritual instinct, which occupies a central position and "approximates it to the God-image."

Jung recognized as real the spiritual need that longs for wholeness, and accepted images of wholeness being offered by the unconscious, rising from the depths of his psychic nature independently of the conscious mind. Spiritual energies from the unconscious serve what he calls the individuation process, whereby one's real self urges one to strive to become who one is intended to be.

The present study is not exhaustive, considering the great number and variety of Jung's "God-words." It is not an attempt to formulate a "Jungian dogma" about God, since Jung stated that it certainly is difficult to discover connecting links between dogma and the immediate experience of psychological archetypes. My approach begins with the question of God's existence by believing or by knowing. Next is the question of whether existence means a Being or energy or spirit, followed by the question of personality. Finally comes the question of how God acts in our lives and how we respond.

The reader's attention is called to the Chronology of Jung's Writings on God on pages 84–95. This includes a table of his writings (1878–1961), followed by explanatory comments.

1

EXISTENCE OF GOD
Knowing or Believing

DOES GOD EXIST? IF, "Yes," what are the physical or mental evidences? In consideration of the limitations of language, existence may be defined as either a physical or psychic reality. It may relate to physical matter or to a mental idea. In his earliest writings on the question of the existence of God, Jung at midlife indicated that the concept of God is simply a necessary psychological function of an irrational nature that has no connection with the question of God's existence. He wrote that it is evident that one cannot conceive God, much less realize that God actually exists, because it is difficult to imagine a process that is not causally conditioned. What preceded God, for example, in order to create God? The existence of God, he said, is once and for all "an absurd problem."[1]

Later, Jung undertook fairly extensive alterations and improvements, including changes in wording on the existence of God, writing that the human intellect can never answer the question and that the physical existence of God is an unanswerable question. He stated that proof is superfluous, because present everywhere is the idea of an all-powerful divine Being, unconsciously if not

[1] "The Psychology of the Unconscious Processes" in *Collected Papers on Analytical Psychology* (1917): pp. 414–415; and in *Two Essays on Analytical Psychology* (CW 7, 1973; edn. 2, 1972): ¶ 110.

consciously, because it is an archetype, a primordial image as an inborn mode of psychic functioning.[2]

Jung emphasized that his psychological observations were not a proof of the existence of God, but proved only the existence of an archetypal "God-image" with the quality of numinosity or awe-inspiring spirit.[3] He took his stand on Kant, which meant that an assertion does not posit its object and that his assertions refer to the psychology of the God-image, which are never metaphysical or pertaining to a real being.[4]

In a letter to a Swiss pastor in 1945 with regard to a question about the God-image being identical with God, Jung replied that there is no justification for such an assumption. He also stated that he would consider it to be extremely dishonest if a psychologist were to assert that the God-image does not have tremendous effect on the psyche.[5]

He went on to say that for a scientist this has nothing to do with the theological question of God's exist-

---

[2] *Two Essays on Analytical Psychology* (1928; German 1926); and in CW 7: ¶ 110.

[3] *Psychology and Religion* (Terry Lectures 1937): p. 73; and CW 11 (1958; edn.2, 1969): ¶ 102. It may be noted that the wording in the original edition was "archetypal image òf the Deity," rather than "God-image"—the latter usage in CW 11 reflecting Jung's insistence later in life that, when he spoke of God, he meant God-image in the psyche.

[4] *C. G. Jung Letters* (1973) vol. 1: p. 294 (8 February 1941 letter to Josef Goldbrunner, Ph.D., Roman Catholic priest, Munich; later, Regensburg).

[5] Psyche, according to Jung's basic definition, is the totality of all psychic processes, conscious as well as unconscious (CW 6: ¶ 797). He viewed the unconscious as an *exclusively psychological* concept, a borderline concept which covers all psychic contents or processes not related to the ego in any perceptible way, including conscious perceptions that can become unconscious through loss of their energic value—this being defined as the *personal unconscious,* which was considered as resting upon the *collective unconscious,* whose contents had never been in consciousness and reflected archetypal processes related to the instinctual bases of the human race. (See *A Critical Dictionary of Jungian Analysis,* p. 155.)

ence, since he was concerned only with the scientific description of psychic dominants or archetypes, whether they be called God, Allah, Buddha, Purusha, Zeus, planets, zodiac, or sex.[6]

In 1951, at age 76, Jung reported that he had been asked so often whether or not he believed in the existence of God that he was somewhat concerned that he be taken for an adherent of "psychologism," meaning that he did not propose any "doctrine" of psychological conceptions to be applied outside the field of psychology proper. He pointed out that what most people seem unable to understand, or that they overlook, is the fact that he regarded the psyche as *real*, whereas they believed only in physical facts. He went on to state that God is an obvious psychic (of the psyche) and non-physical fact, a fact that can be established psychically but not physically.[7]

In a letter in 1955 from a man asking why he (the man) believed so confidently in the existence of God, Jung replied that nobody could really tell him why; it was just a fact, for reasons unknown. Jung stated that God is an immediate experience of a very primordial nature, one of the most natural products of our mental life, as birds sing, as wind whistles, as the surf thunders. He pointed out that people who think that they know reasons for everything are oblivious to the fact that the existence of the universe, itself, is one big unfathomable secret, and so is our human existence.[8]

---

[6] *Letters,* vol. 1: pp. 360–361 (7 April 1945 letter to Max Frischknecht, Pastor, Basel).

[7] *Answer to Job* (1954; German 1952); and CW 11 (1958; edn. 2, 1969): ¶ 751.

[8] *Letters,* vol. 2: pp. 252–253 (7 May 1955 letter to B. A. Snowdon, Brighton, England).

Jung acknowledged in a newspaper interview in 1955 that all that he had learned had led him step by step to an unshakable conviction of the existence of God and that one can experience God every day. He emphasized that he could only believe in what he knew, which eliminates believing. Therefore, he said, he did not take God's existence on belief—he *knew* that God exists.[9]

Jung's distinction between believing and knowing caused considerable discussion after his "Face to Face" interview for BBC television in 1959, when he was asked by John Freeman about his religious upbringing and if he believed in God as a child, to which he replied, "Oh, yes." In answer to the question whether he believed in God *now,* he paused, then replied, "Difficult to answer. I *know.* I don't need to believe. I know."[10]

So many letters were received by Jung that emphasized his statement about "knowing" God that he wrote to the producer of the Freeman interview and enclosed a copy of his letter to a man whose letter was "particularly articulate." Jung wrote that he had explained what his opinion was about a "knowledge of God" and explained that he knew it was an unconventional way of thinking, and that he understood it should suggest that he was "no Christian." However, he added, "Yet I think of myself as a Christian, since I am based entirely upon Christian concepts."[11]

---

[9] *C. G. Jung Speaking* (1977): pp. 250–251 ("Men, Women, and God," interview for London *Daily Mail*, 1955).

[10] *C. G. Jung Speaking* (1977): pp. 427–428 ("Face to Face" interview, 1959).

[11] *Letters,* vol. 2: p. 524 (5 Dec. 1959 letter to Hugh Burnett, BBC producer of the John Freeman "Face to Face" interview with Jung in October).

Jung commented in his letter to the "articulate writer" that Mr. Freeman fired the question at him in a somewhat surprising way, so that he was perplexed and had to say the next thing which came to mind. He remarked that, as soon as he answered, he knew he had said something controversial, puzzling, or even ambiguous, and went on to say that he didn't say, "There is a God," but had said he didn't need to believe in God, he *knew*, which did not mean that he knew a certain God (Zeus, Yahweh, Allah, etc.), but rather that he did know that he was obviously confronted with a factor unknown in itself, which he called "God." He added that he *knew* of his "collision" with a superior will in his own psychic system—*he knew of God*, just as much dwelling in himself as everywhere else.[12]

One of Jung's last "summary" statements about God was published by H. L. Philp in his book *Jung and the Problem of Evil* (1958), which contained correspondence between Philp and Jung in the format of questions and answers. In answer to the question as to whether or not Jung believed in the existence of God other than as an archetype, which Philp felt that Jung had not actually answered in *Answer to Job*, Jung replied:

> We find numberless images of God, but we cannot produce the original. There is no doubt in my mind that there is an original behind our images, but it is inaccessible. We could not even be aware of the original since its translation into psychic

---

[12] *Letters*, vol. 2: pp. 525–526 (5 Dec. 1959 letter to M. Leonard, King's College, Newcastle upon Tyne).

terms is necessary in order to make it perceptible at all. . . . Why should we be so immodest as to suppose that we could catch a universal being in the narrow confines of our language? We know that God-images play a great role in psychology, but we cannot prove the physical existence of God. As a responsible scientist I am not going to preach my personal and subjective convictions which I cannot prove. . . . Speaking for myself, the question whether God exists or not is futile. I am sufficiently convinced of the effects man has always attributed to a divine being. If I should express a belief beyond that or should assert the existence of God, it would not only be superfluous and inefficient, it would show that I am not basing my opinion on facts. When people say that they believe in the existence of God, it has never impressed me in the least. Either I know a thing and then I don't need to believe it; or I believe it because I am not sure that I know it. I am well satisfied with the fact that I know experiences which I cannot avoid calling numinous or divine."[13]

Commenting early on about the physical existence of God, as stated in 1938 in his seminar on Nietzsche's *Zarathustra*, Jung observed that Nietzsche thought that someone once said that God existed, but naturally, when that someone did not prove it nor bring any evidence, it meant to Nietzsche that God was not. Jung hearkened back to the old understanding that somewhere—perhaps

---

[13] H. L. Philp, *Jung and the Problem of Evil*, pp. 15–16; and in CW 18: ¶ 1589.

behind the galactic system—God was sitting on a throne and if one used a telescope one might perhaps discover God; otherwise there was no God. He pointed out that neither stones nor plants nor arguments nor theologians prove God's existence. Only human consciousness reveals God as a fact, because it is a fact that there is an idea of a divine being in the human psyche.[14]

With regard to "where" God is, Jung, in his last published writing in *Man and His Symbols* (1961), observed that, "Because we cannot discover God's throne in the sky with a radio telescope . . . people assume that such ideas are 'not true.'" He would rather say that they are not "true" *enough,* because such conceptions have been a part of human life from prehistoric times and still break through into consciousness at any provocation.[15]

Jung wrote to an American professor in 1960 that he insisted on dealing with psychic phenomena and not with metaphysical assertions with regard to Martin Buber's accusations.[16] Stating that he was not concerned with the truth or untruth of God's existence, Jung emphasized that he was "concerned with the statement only," and was interested in its structure and behavior, given that he had found within the frame of psychic events the belief in God which says: "God is." He pointed out that the statement is an emotionally-toned complex, like the father- or mother-complex, and that it is obvious that if humans did not exist, no statement could exist either, nor could anyone prove that the statement "God" exists in a nonhuman sphere.

---

[14] *Nietzsche's Zarathustra: Notes of the Seminar Given in 1934–1939 by C. G. Jung* (1988): p. 1352 (lecture on 19 October 1938).

[15] *Man and His Symbols* (1961): p. 87.

[16] *Letters,* vol. 2: pp. 570–572 (29 June 1960 letter to Robert C. Smith, Villanova, PA; later, professor at Trenton State College, New Jersey).

Buber, having no practical experience in depth psychology, did not know of the easily observable fact of the "autonomy of complexes," whereas the autonomous God-complex was a subject confronting him. Jung's concern, however, was with the practical and theoretical problem of how-do-complexes-behave, and particularly how the God-complex behaves in different individuals and societies.

Continuing with his answer to Buber, Jung's psychological argument was that "God," within the frame of psychology, is an autonomous complex, a "dynamic" image in the psyche, and that is all psychology is ever able to state. It cannot know more about God. He commented, with irony, that Buber, "as a theologian," had far more information about God's "true existence" and other of God's qualities than Jung could ever dream of acquiring, and that Jung's ambitions did not soar to theological heights. Psychologists cannot prove or disprove God's actual existence, he said, but they do know how fallible images in the human mind are.

He wrote that, "If I talk of the God-image I do not deny a transcendental reality," and he "merely" insisted on the psychic reality of the God-complex or the God-image. He cited Nobel Prize winner-physicist Niels Bohr's proposed analogy of the model of atomic structure with a planetary system, knowing that it was a model of a transcendent and unknown reality. Jung commented that Bohr would not be as dumb as to believe that his model was an exact and true replica of the atom, and that no empiricist in his senses would believe his models to be the eternal truth itself.

2

ESSENCE OF GOD
Being or Substance

I F GOD EXISTS, WHAT IS
God's "essence"? Essence has many definitions, among
which are metaphysical substance, totality of attributes,
necessary constituents, ground of existence, fundamental
or intrinsic being, and quality of substance in nature. It.
seems to follow upon a discussion of the existence of God.
Wholeness or unity is the original condition of existence,
before the first "thought" enters and begins to discriminate and differentiate "this" from "that."

Jung's speculations on the essential nature of God
ranged from permanent being to matter or substance, and
energy. The fundamental or intrinsic nature of God as operative as "God-image" in the depths of the psyche of human beings and as unprovable "God" transcendent to the
universe constantly occupied his thinking. He wrote in
1948 that he made use of a God-concept (or of an equally
metaphysical concept of energy) because these images have
been found in the human psyche from the beginning.[1]

In a letter to a Swiss pastor in 1945, he observed that
the "great incompatibles," such as being and non-being,
person and non-person, and the union of opposites, in
general, belong to the picture of "the divine paradox."[2]

---

[1] "General Aspects of the Psychology of the Dream" in *Spring* 1956: p. 23, from
original German of 1948; and in CW 8 (1960; edn. 2, 1969): ¶ 528.
[2] *C. G. Jung Letters* (1973), vol. 1: p. 392 (20 Nov. 1945 letter to H. Wegmann,
pastor, Zurich).

In his *Answer to Job* (1952), Jung wrote that, "whenever we speak of religious contents we move in a world of images that point to something ineffable," that is, incapable of being expressed in words. And we do not know how clear or unclear images, metaphors, and concepts are in respect to their transcendental "object." In saying the word "God," he said, we express a verbal concept or image that has undergone changes in time, and we do not know whether such changes affect "only the concepts and images, or the Unspeakable itself." He added, "After all, we can imagine God as an eternally flowing current of vital energy that endlessly changes shape just as easily as we can image him as an eternally unmoved, unchangeable essence."[3]

Jung places a great deal of emphasis on the fact that statement and image are psychic processes—and are different from their transcendental object; that is, they do not posit it or locate it in relation to other objects, they merely point to it. In fact, it is impossible to demonstrate God's reality to oneself except by using statements or images that have arisen spontaneously or are sanctified by tradition. He pointed to the naive-minded person who has never separated psychic images from their unknowable metaphysical background.[4]

GOD AS BEING

Considering Jung's statements that God, as such, is unknowable and ineffable, he said almost nothing about God

---

[3] *Answer to Job.* p. xii; and CW 11: ¶ 555.
[4] *Answer to Job.* p. xviii; and CW 11: ¶ 558.

as being, which has a number of definitions, such as presence or actuality. He spoke of psychic reality. He did mention God as the "unfathomable Being" in his essay on the spirit Mercurius (1942). In commenting on the word "God" in the foreword to Victor White's *God and the Unconscious* (1952), he observed that theologians naturally assume that the metaphysical *Ens Absolutum* ("absolute being") is meant. Empiricists do not dream of making such a far-reaching assumption, he said, or at most they may mean an archetypal motif that prefigures such statements. For them "God" could just as well mean Yahweh, Allah, Shiva, etc.[5]

In his thesis on synchronicity (an acausal connecting principle of meaningful coincidence), Jung wrote in the same year of a "unity of being" which would have to be expressed in a new conceptual language, that is, a "neutral language," as physicist Wolfgang Pauli once called it. Jung's comment followed his question about a viewpoint that the latest conclusions of science were coming ever nearer to a unitary idea of being, characterized by space and time on one hand and by causality and synchronicity on the other.[6] These comments seem to relate to his statement in the conclusion to his study of "A Psychological Approach to the Dogma of the Trinity" (1940) that "God is pure reality."[7]

The spiritual concept of "being" was expressed as universal being in Jung's studies of oriental philosophies and religion, as in his commentary on *The Secret of the*

---

[5] Victor White, *God and the Unconscious*, p. xix; and CW 11: ¶ 454.

[6] C. G. Jung and Wolfgang Pauli, *The Interpretation of Nature and the Psyche*, (1955: p. 240; German 1952); and in CW 8: ¶ 960.

[7] "Zur Psychologie der Trinitatsidee" in *Eranos-Jahrbuch 1940/41*; and in CW 11: ¶ 289.

Golden Flower, in which he included the idea of a universal being in Taoist concepts.[8] He also commented on impressions he had during his visit to India in 1937–38 about the varied simplicity of Indian life as grounded in the "All and All-Oneness of Universal Being," including his encounter with a "little holy man" who had found meaning in Being as an example of wisdom, holiness, *and* humanity.[9]

GOD AS ENERGY

Jung's writings on the essence of God as energy appeared as early as 1912, at age 37, which was published in English in 1916 as *Psychology of the Unconscious.* He wrote, "God is to be considered as the representative of a certain sum of energy (libido)," which then appears projected because it works from the unconscious outward.[10] In 1952 he added that he was of the opinion that, in general, one worships the psychic force within the psyche as something divine and that psychic energy of libido creates the God-image by making use of archetypal patterns.[11] He observed in 1933 (*The Visions Seminars*) that "God is the supreme force in a person's psychology, the supreme and ultimately decisive factor."[12]

---

[8] "Commentary" in *The Secret of the Golden Flower,* translated and explained by Richard Wilhelm, with foreword and commentary by C. G. Jung (1931; German 1929); and in CW 13: ¶ 59.

[9] Original essay, "Uber den indischen Heiligen," in Heinrich Zimmer's *Der Weg zum Selbst* (1944); and as "The Holy Men of India" in CW 11: ¶ 952–953.

[10] Original in *Wandlungen und Symbole der Libido* (1912; English edition as *Psychology of the Unconscious* in 1916; reprinted in 1992 as supplementary volume B of *The Collected Works of C. G. Jung*): ¶ 111; and in CW 5 as *Symbols of Transformation*: ¶ 89.

[11] *Symbols of Transformation* (CW 5, 1956): ¶ 129 (original in German, 1952).

[12] *The Visions Seminars* (1976: p. 366; lecture given in 1933, originally published in *Spring* 1969: p. 18).

In 1931, Jung discussed problems confronting psychology that did not appeal to the physical world as a ground for explanation, but rather appealed to a spiritual system whose active principle is neither matter nor any state of energy, but God. He went on to speculate that psychologists might be tempted by "nature philosophy" to call energy or the *elan vital* (vital force or impulse) God and thereby blend spirit and nature into one. He commented that if he were to recognize only naturalistic values ("everything in physical terms"), he would hinder or even destroy the spiritual development of his patients. And, contrariwise, if he would hold exclusively to a spiritual interpretation, he would violate the person's right to exist as a physical being. He concluded by saying that he must be able to give appropriate psychological explanations, for how could he know "whether energy is God or God is energy."[13]

According to Jung, the idea of energy and its conservation must be a primordial image dormant in the depths of the collective unconscious, and this concept of power was the earliest form of a concept of God among primitives. It has undergone countless variations in the course of history, such as magic power glowing in the burning bush and in the countenance of Moses in the Old Testament, and as fiery tongues from heaven descending with the Holy Ghost in the New Testament. He also explained that, "If, for instance, I make use of a God-concept or an equally metaphysical concept of energy, I do so because

---

[13] "Basic Postulates of Analytical Psychology" in *Modern Man in Search of a Soul* (1933): pp. 188–189 (original in German, 1931); and in CW 8 (1960; edn.2, 1969): ¶ 678.

they are images which have been found in the human psyche from the beginning."[14]

GOD AS SUBSTANCE OR MATTER

Jung's observations of the essence of God as being matter included his statement in 1936 that the alchemists came to project even the highest value, namely God, into matter.[15] In 1946, however, he stated that the *prima materia* was not to be understood as God; and he added in a footnote that the identification of the *prima materia* with God occurred not only in alchemy, but in other branches of medieval philosophy as well.[16]

God is spirit, as Jung pointed out in a lecture in 1935, and "spirit to us is nothing substantial or dynamic." But, he went on to say that, if one studies the original meaning of these terms, one gets at the real nature of the underlying experience. Then one understands how they affect the primitive mind, and, in a similar way, the "primitive psyche in ourselves." Since spirit, *spiritus* (Latin), or *pneuma* (Greek) really means breath or air, and one is moved by them as by a wind, then in its archetypal character, it is a dynamic agent and "half-substantial."[17] In a lecture in 1945, Jung defined spirit as an immaterial

---

[14] "On the Psychology of the Unconscious" in CW 7: ¶ 108 (see Ch. 1, note 2, above).

[15] "Religious Ideas in Alchemy" in *Psychology and Alchemy* (1953) as CW 12: ¶ 432 (original in German as *Psychologie und Alchemie*, 1944).

[16] "The Psychology of the Transference" in *Psychology and Alchemy* (1953) as CW 16: ¶ 533 [original in German as *Die Psychologie der Ubertragung*, 1946]

[17] *Analytical Psychology; Its Theory and Practice. The Tavistock Lectures* at The Institute of Medical Psychology, London, 1935 (publ. 1968) p. 174; and in CW 18: ¶ 359.

"substance" or form of existence, which on the highest and most universal level is called "God." He imagined this immaterial substance also as the "vehicle of psychic phenomena or even of life itself."[18]

Jung remarked in 1939 in his psychological commentary on *The Tibetan Book of the Great Liberation,* that, whether one calls the principle of existence "God," "matter," "energy," or anything else, one has created nothing; one has simply changed a symbol.[19] However, symbols are extremely important, and among these in reference to God, he said, are the circle and the quaternity. He wrote in 1940, for example, that since olden times the circle with a center has been a symbol of the Deity, illustrating the wholeness of God.[20] He observed in the Terry lectures on *Psychology and Religion* (1937) that, through the use of comparative method, it had been shown without a doubt that the quaternity (union of four in one, such as the four sides of a square) is a more or less "direct representation of the God who is manifest in creation." Moreover, he remarked that one might conclude, therefore, that such a symbol, spontaneously produced in dreams of modern people, means something similar—*the God within.*[21]

---

[18] "The Phenomenology of the Spirit in Fairy Tales" (Eranos lecture, 1945); published in *Spirit and Nature,* Papers from the Eranos Yearbooks, 1 (1954); and in CW 9, Part I: ¶ 385 (original in German as "Zur Psychologie des Geistes" in *Eranos-Jahrbuch,* 1945).

[19] "Psychological Commentary" written in English in 1939 for *The Tibetan Book of the Great Liberation* (1954): p. xxxi; and in CW 11: ¶ 763.

[20] "Transformation Symbolism in the Mass" (Eranos lecture, 1940), published in *The Mysteries,* Papers from the Eranos Yearbooks, 2 (1955); and in CW 11: ¶ 418 (original in German as "Das Wandlungssymbol in der Messe" in *Eranos-Jahrbuch* 1940/41).

[21] *Psychology and Religion* (The Terry Lectures, Yale, 1937), p. 72; and in CW 11: ¶ 101.

3

PERSONALITY OF GOD
Persona and Shadow

F̶OLLOWING CONSIDER-
ations of the "essence of God" comes interest in the attributes, characteristics, and qualities of God as reflected in
images of God—the God-images in the psyches of human
beings. What are the material and spiritual peculiarities
that comprise one's acquaintanceship with God? From the
point of view of most of the world's religions, "God"
takes on the form of a super-human being, with a "personality" attached. As Jung said, "How the people of the Old
Testament felt about their God we know from the testi-
mony of the Bible."[1]

In connection with the idea of the personification of
God, Jung wrote (in a letter to a Swiss pastor in 1959)
that the distance between God and man is so great that
Yahweh saw himself obliged to set up an embassy among
his people—the ambassador being his own son—in order
to deliver a missive to them, the gospel.[2] This was related
to the concept that the Israelites had made their God king
in the wilderness, which gave rise to the concept of a
"kingdom of God," as in Exodus 19:6, Daniel 2:44, and
numerous references in the New Testament. Moreover,
Jung suggested that the idea of a special incarnation of

---

[1] *Answer to Job* (1954): p. 3; and *Religion and Psychology: West and East* (CW 11, 1952; edn. 2, 1969): ¶ 561.

[2] *Letters,* vol. 2: p. 483 (12 February 1959 letter to Swiss pastor, Tanner).

God in Jesus resulted in the scourging, the crowning with thorns, and the clothing in a purple robe, which "show Jesus as the archaic sacrificed king." He also suggested that the punishment was carried out on God, the model for the execution being the ritual slaying of the king, which referred to the archaic practice of the king being killed in order to improve the condition of his people when he showed signs of impotence and failure, just as God was sacrificed "for the salvation of mankind." Jung goes on to say that, for primitive man, the actual king was suited perfectly to this purpose, but not for a higher level of civilization with a more spiritual conception of God.[3]

If one considers cosmogony (origin and development of the universe) and wonders about the creation, origin, or manner of coming into existence of our world and of ourselves, one may ponder Jung's statement in his letter to a Swiss woman in 1957: "Coming now to cosmogony, we can assert nothing except that the body of the world and its psyche are a reflection of the God we imagine." He reiterated that we cannot speak of "God," but only of a God-image, which we make, or which appears to us from the unconscious, and we can project only a conception of God that corresponds to our own constitution, which involves a body perceived by the senses and a "spirit (= psyche)" directly conscious of itself. In other words, one is dealing with the anthropomorphism of God in human form or/and with human attributes and affections (emotions).[4]

---

[3] "Transformation Symbolism in the Mass" (Eranos lecture, 1940), published in *The Mysteries: Papers from the Eranos Yearbooks,* 2 (1955): pp. 332–335; and in CW 11: ¶ 406–409.

[4] *Letters,* vol. 2: 342 (2 January 1957 letter to Dr. N.).

Although it is difficult to view God in human form rationally, given the concept that "man was created in God's image," it seems equally as difficult to find God's form in a certain place. Therefore, one is left with the caution, as Jung stated many times, that it is only through the psyche that we can experience God by way of the God-image. Jung wrote in 1935 that to assert that God is absolute means placing God outside all connection with human beings and that an absolute God "does not concern us in the least, whereas a 'psychological' God would be *real*" and could reach us.[5] Quoting Goethe:

> The Highest bliss on earth shall be
> The joys of personality![6]

in a lecture delivered in 1932, Jung commented that it expressed the view that the ultimate aim and strongest desire of everyone lie in developing the "fullness of human existence that is called personality."[7] Personality may be defined as a totality of individual characteristics or as identity, or as an integrative group of instinctual trends, interests, and behavioral tendencies. Consequently, Jung's view of "God," and particularly of "Yahweh," reflected a comparison of the existence of persona and shadow complexes in

---

[5] "The Relations between the Ego and the Unconscious" in *Two Essays in Analytical Psychology* (CW 7): ¶ 394 note.

[6] Goethe, Johann Wolfgang von. *"West-Eastern Divan/West-79 Oestlicher Divan*, trans. by J. Wheley (London: Oswald Wolff Publishers, 1974). C. G. Jung: *The Development of the Personality* (Princeton: Princeton University Press, 1954): p. 167; and in CW 17, ¶ 284.

[7] "The Development of Personality" in *The Integration of the Personality* (1939): p. 281; and in CW 17: ¶ 284 [original in German as "Vom Werden der Personlichkeit" in *Wirklichkeit der Seele*, 1934].

humanity as in the Creator. "Persona" refers to the external face or mask of personality that exists for reasons of adaptation or personal convenience, and is by no means identical with individuality. "Shadow" refers to the negative side of the personality as the total of all unpleasant qualities one wants to hide.

Jung's controversial writings in his *Answer to Job* (1952) reflect a strong anthromorphic impression, i.e., a representation or conception of God in super-human form, or with human attributes and affections. He commented on "the powerful personality of Yahweh," and he added that Yahweh lacked biographical antecedents, having "no origin and no past, except his creation of the world, with which all history began."[8]

ATTRIBUTES

Jung, in considering the standpoint of past ages, wrote in an essay in 1931 that the individual soul is dependent on a spiritual world-system, which assumed that this system was a being with a will and consciousness, "even a person," calling this being God, "the quintessence of reality, the most real of beings, the first cause."[9] In 1928 he also referred to the First Cause, in which he posed the paradox of all instinctual forces being opposed to the spiritual principle because it asserted the essential contradictoriness of the God-concept as one and the same being, whose "inner-

---

[8] *Answer to Job:* p. 17; and in CW 11: ¶ 576.
[9] "Basic Postulates of Analytical Psychology" in *Modern Man in Search of a Soul* (1933): 187–188; and in CW 8: ¶ 677 [original in German as "Die Entschleierung der Seele," 1931].

most nature is a tension of opposites." He goes on to point out that science calls this "being" energy, because energy is like a "living balance between opposites." He also stated:

> Thus God would be not only the spiritual light, appearing as the latest flower on the tree of evolution, nor only the spiritual goal of redemption in which all creation culminates, not only the end and purpose, but also the darkest, primordial cause of nature's blackest deeps. This is a tremendous paradox which manifestly corresponds to a profound psychological truth.[10]

Jung cautioned, in his Zarathustra seminar in 1936, that "God never was invented," but was always an occurrence, a psychological experience, and still is. But, in the 19th century, conditions were particularly unfavorable because people had assumptions about God from their conscious thinking. And, since God was an object of worship, something definite must be said about God.[11] These attributes from Christian doctrine included *omnipresence* (being in all places and things), *omnipotence* (powerful over all things), *omniscience* (knowing all things), *immutability* (unchangeable and unalterable), *eternal* (existing without beginning or ending), *creator and preserver of the world, and morally perfect being*. When one speculates on attributes of God, one may reflect on the practice in Islam of

---

[10] "On Psychical Energy" in *Contributions to Analytical Psychology* (1928): pp. 62–63; and in CW 8: ¶ 103 with slight change in wording.
[11] *Nietzche's Zarathustra: Notes of the Seminar Given in 1934–1939 by C. G. Jung* (1988): p. 916 (lecture on 13 May 1936).

addressing Allah in prayer by 99 names, which may suggest *omni* (Latin for "all").

Jung commented on many of these attributes, but not in a systematic way. For example, he remarked in his Zarathustra seminar regarding God as the infinite or eternal one, like the dogmatic Christian formulation, that such a quality is an "absolutely manmade assumption" and reaches beyond the limits of the human mind.[12] In response to a question from a Swiss teacher (1955), he spoke of an evolving God, that there was greater consensus on the basis of mythological knowledge for that assumption than for the belief in an unchanging, immovable God (*Deus immobilis*). He added that even Yahweh, the Old Testament God "who lacked a personal biography," created a temporal world and was allied to a chosen people and then later changed his character, thereby changing from an eternal to an historical figure.[13]

One should be reminded here of Jung's basic statement that, when he speaks of God, or of Yahweh in this instance, he always means a *God-image* within the human psyche.

• • •

In assuming that God, in terms of the anthropomorphism that the human mind projects, exhibits consciousness, Jung wrote that when one considers the data of paleontology with the view that "a conscious creator has perhaps

---

[12] *Nietzche's Zarathustra*: p. 927 (lecture of 20 May 1936).
[13] *Letters*, vol. 2: p. 250 (2 May 1955 letter to Walter Robert Corti, Swiss writer, philosopher, teacher).

spent a thousand million years," and seems to have made many detours to produce consciousness, he concluded that God had not an absolute unconsciousness, but a "rather dim consciousness." From this idea he concludes that such a consciousness necessarily would produce "any number of errors and impasses with the most cruel consequences, disease, mutilation, and horrible fights."[14]

OPPOSITES

Among Jung's latest writings was a letter to an American medical student in 1961 (a few months before his death), in which Jung observed that the monotheistic tendency "always tries to postulate or to construct an anthropomorphic unity of the God-image," and that such a God-image is paradoxical or contradictory. Such a unity, he said, is "strange and painful to us." These comments were made in response to the problem of Job, whose fundamental fact was the pair of opposites united in the image of God (i.e., Yahweh). The pair of opposites are love and fear, Jung said, which presuppose an apparently irreconcilable contradiction. He goes on to say:

> Yet such an opposition must be expected whenever we are confronted with an immense energy. There is no dynamic manifestation without a corresponding initial tension which provided the necessary energy. If we suppose the deity to be a dynamic phenomenon in our experience, its origin must be

---

[14] *Letters,* vol. 2: p. 312 (30 June 1956 letter to Dr. Elined Kotschnig, Jungian analyst, Washington, DC).

an opposition or a paradox. Job obviously is confronted with this problem and he even expresses his conviction that God will help him against God. . . . If we try to realize what the full acceptance of such an image means, we will soon discover why most people are afraid of it."[15]

If one accepts the concept of an all-encompassing God, if God is held to be a *coincidencia oppositorum* (coincidence of opposites), which Nicholas of Cusa (1401–1464) identified with God, Jung pointed out that such a concept of an all-encompassing God just necessarily includes opposites, but that such coincidences must not be too extreme, "otherwise God would cancel himself out," as he lectured in 1942.[16] He used that term or the term *complexio oppositorum* many times in his writing.

In reply to a letter in 1955 from a Swiss philosopher asking what one can assert about God, Jung wrote that the answer probably would be only contradictory principles. These would include God as creator of both supreme light and gloomiest abyss, and uniting both genesis and decay. Another contradiction would be God as infinite, yet finite as personality. He confessed, in viewing the union of all opposites, "There are some who, faced with these illimitabilities, can escape to the floating island of belief, take to the lifeboat of the graced, but I have never belonged to their number."[17]

---

[15] *Letters*, vol. 2: p. 623 (19 January 1961 letter to Michael A. Ledeen, medical student, Claremont, CA).

[16] *The Spirit Mercury* (printed 1953 for private circulation; original in German as "Der Geist Mercurius" in *Eranos-Jahrbuch 1942*, and in *Symbolik des Geistes*, 1948); in *Alchemical Studies* (CW 13, 1967): ¶ 256.

[17] *Letters*, vol. 2: p. 249 (2 May 1955 letter to Swiss educator Walter Robert Corti).

PERSONALITY IN *THE BOOK OF JOB*

Jung's experience in writing *Answer to Job* (1952) represented the culmination of a lifetime of questions about God, and resulted in considerable criticism, particularly from theologians. In spite of his claim that he was writing about the God-image rather than "God himself," and despite his statement later in life (1959), Jung wrote, in response to a friendly letter, that whatever he said in the book did not refer to "God himself, but rather to the idea or opinion man makes of God."[18]

Nevertheless, the "problem," from a "statistical" point of view, was that Jung used the words "God-image" or *imago Dei* or image of God only eleven times in *Job*, in contrast to the word "God," which he used nearly four hundred times and "Yahweh," which he used one hundred and sixty times. Consequently, one may wonder about Jung's language in *Job*, when he frequently used both God and Yahweh in the same paragraph and occasionally in the same sentence. The phrases "God's marriage with Israel" and "Yahweh's marriage with Israel" in consecutive paragraphs illustrate this "problem." On most pages of the "little book," both "God" and "Yahweh" are there.

The basic problem in responding to Jung's statement that when he spoke of God he always meant God-image, was that he wrote in a letter to a Swiss pastor in 1955, stating that "In *Job* and elsewhere I am always explicitly speaking of the *God-image*" and that, "I speak of the *God-image and not of God* because it is quite beyond me to say anything about God at all."[19]

---

[18] *Letters,* vol. 2: p. 526 (23 December 1959 letter to Mary Louise Ainsworth, Berkeley, CA).

[19] *Letters,* vol. 2: p. 260 (13 June 1955 letter to Walter Bernet, pastor, Bern, Switzerland).

Nevertheless, the substitution of "God-image" for every mention of the word "God" in *Answer to Job* would be a monumental task, even if one constantly kept in mind that "God" and "Yahweh" would be anthropomorphic images in the person's psyche. And the personification of God and/or Yahweh is inevitable; and, in analyzing *Job*, one needs to keep in mind that the account written by the author of the Book of Job reflected the prevailing psychological state of projection of human values onto the mysterious "other." Although authorship of the *Book of Job* was probably composite, it probably being written in the second millennium B.C. (between 1600–1050 B.C.), the "dialogue" (chapters 3–31) definitely shows the influence of a single (poetic) personality in one of the great masterpieces of world literature.

Jung's own use of "God" and "Yahweh" in *Answer to Job* and their characterization as masculine represented his own religious background. In writing to an Episcopal rector in 1958 with regard to *Answer to Job*, Jung stated, "As you realize, I am discussing the admittedly anthropomorphic image of Yahweh and I do not apply metaphysical judgments." He added:

> The absence of human morality in Yahweh is a stumbling block which cannot be overlooked. . . . We miss reason and moral values, that is, two main characteristics of a mature human mind. It is therefore obvious that the Yahwistic image or conception of the deity is less than certain human specimens: the image of a personified brutal force and of an unethical and non-spiritual mind, yet in-

consistent enough to exhibit traits of kindness and generosity besides a violent power-drive. . . . This image owes its existence certainly not to an invention of intellectual formulation but rather to a spontaneous manifestation, i.e., to religious experience of men like Samuel and Job. . . . People still ask: Is it possible that God allows such things?"[20]

In terms of the "personality" of Yahweh/God in *Job,* Jung dealt primarily with Yahweh's behavior from the points of view of morality, justice, injustice, fear, and love, especially within the context of antinomy (lit., against law; contradiction between two principles, each of which is taken to be true). He commented that Yahweh was persecutor and helper in one, that his divided attitude put human beings in an impossible position, that his dual nature remained hidden from himself alone, and that Yahweh breathed his own mystery into Creation, which meant that all possibilities were contained in him.

Jung also used "God" in the same way, as in his comments that Job realized God's inner antinomy, that Job recognized God's contradictory nature, that Job had seen God's face and the unconscious split in God's nature, that all opposites were of God so that humanity must bend to that burden, and that God's oppositeness had been incarnated in human beings, who become vessels filled with divine conflict. He poetically characterized, in his analysis of the Apocalypse, the Revelation of John, that God has a

---

[20] *Letters,* vol. 2: pp. 434–435 (3 May 1958 letter to Morton T. Kelsey, Episcopal priest, Monrovia, CA).

terrible double aspect: "a sea of grace is met by a seething lake of fire." He added that the paradoxical nature of God has an effect on human beings as a seemingly insoluble conflict.[21]

•　•　•

Jung's thesis in *Answer to Job,* assuming the author of the *Book of Job's* characterization of an anthropomorphic personality of Israel's god, Yahweh, was that Yahweh's powerful personality demonstrated a lack of consciousness. He commented on Yahweh as a *phenomenon* and, as Job said, "not a man," which indicated that Yahweh's behavior was that of an unconscious being who could not be judged morally.[22] His behavior, up to the reappearance of Sophia, Jung wrote, as a whole was accompanied by an inferior consciousness which was not much more than a primitive "awareness" which knew no reflection, i.e., psychologically "unconscious."[23] He speculated that the immediate cause of the Incarnation lay in Job's elevation and that its purpose was the differentiation of Yahweh's consciousness.[24] He stated that Yahweh's behavior after the Job episode brought about a curious change, that it was "not unthinkable" that the knowledge of his dealing so harshly with Job brought him to the position that he himself should "become conscious of something through this conflict" with Job and thus gain new insight.[25]

---

[21] *Answer to Job* (1954): pp. 10, 23–24, 35, 45, 54, 62, 89, 146, 151); and in CW 11: ¶ 567, 584, 586, 604, 617, 623, 630, 659, 733, 738.

[22] *Answer to Job* (1954): p. 33; and CW 11: ¶ 600.

[23] *Answer to Job* (1954): p. 67; and CW 11: ¶ 632.

[24] *Answer to Job* (1954): p. 70; and CW 11: ¶ 642.

[25] *Answer to Job* (1954): pp. 67–68; and CW 11: ¶ 639.

Jung observed early in *Job* that if Yahweh had been really conscious of himself, he would at least have put an end to the eulogizing on his justice; but he was too unconscious to be moral. Morality, he said, presupposes consciousness. He added that Yahweh was everything in its totality, and therefore, among other things, Yahweh was total justice, and also its total opposite.[26]

Continuing with the concept of Yahweh's "personality" in the context of the *projection* (the act of externalizing or objectifying one's own subjective view) of anthropomorphic characteristics by the author of the Book of Job, Jung analyzed the Job story in terms of why the experiment of testing Job's faithfulness was made and what were the consequences of the "bet with Satan." He commented: "It is amazing to see how easily Yahweh, quite without reason, had let himself be influenced by one of his sons [Satan], by a *doubting thought,* and made unsure of Job's faithfulness." And, he continued: "It is indeed no edifying spectacle to see how quickly Yahweh abandons his faithful servant to the evil spirit and lets him fall without compunction or pity into the abyss of physical and moral suffering." He speculated that Yahweh may have had some secret resistance against Job, possibly something humans have that God does not have, such as a somewhat keener consciousness based on self-reflection.[27]

Therefore, Jung wondered, what would explain Job's sufferings (loss of his children and of all property, as well as wracking illness) and why the "divine wager" with Satan should suddenly come to an end with Yahweh's "speechifying and impressive performance given by the

---

[26] *Answer to Job* (1954): pp. 14–15; and CW 11: ¶ 574.
[27] *Answer to Job* (1954): pp. 19–20; and CW 11: ¶ 579.

prehistoric menagerie" to impress Job of Yahweh's superior power? Jung commented that, shrewdly, Job took up Yahweh's aggressive words and prostrated himself at Yahweh's feet in recognition of the reality of Yahweh's power. The poet in the Book of Job ended with Job's final answer: that his questions had not been answered, but that he had come to understand that Yahweh cannot be called to account. However, Job had experienced the mystery for himself, rather than by hearsay, and bowed down before the Almighty. He had no alternative but to formally revoke his demand for justice from Yahweh.[28]

Jung came to the conclusion that "Without Yahweh's knowledge and contrary to his intentions, the tormented though guiltless Job had secretly been lifted up to a superior knowledge of God [Yahweh] which God [Yahweh] himself did not possess." He added that, if Yahweh had consulted his omniscience, he would not have been at a disadvantage of Job. Jung went on to say that Yahweh in his omniscience could have known how incongruous were his attempts to intimidate Job and must have seen that Job's loyalty was unshakable and that Satan had lost out. Also, Yahweh did not think of bringing Satan to account nor to give Job at least moral satisfaction. And, by recognizing Yahweh's contradictory nature, Job assigned a place to Yahweh's justice and goodness.[29]

As a consequence of the confrontational drama between Job and Yahweh, Jung came to the conclusion: "Yahweh must become man precisely because he had done man a wrong. . . . Because his creature has surpassed him

---

[28] *Answer to Job* (1954): pp. 27, 29, 31–32; and CW 11: ¶ 588, 595, 599.
[29] *Answer to Job* (1954): pp. 22–25; and CW 11: ¶ 583–587.

he must regenerate himself." Jung commented that "Yahweh's intention to become man, which resulted from his collision with Job, is fulfilled in Christ's life and suffering," that Yahweh then identified with his light aspect, becoming the good God and loving father. However, Jung added that Yahweh had not lost his wrath and could still mete out punishment, but he did it with justice.[30]

· · ·

In the latter half of Jung's *Answer to Job,* he employed almost entirely the word "God" rather than "Yahweh," in which he dealt with how matters stood with the Incarnation after the death of Christ, the doctrine of salvation, John and the Apocalypse, and the dogma of the Assumption of Mary, Mother of God. As a kind of sequel to Job's story, Jung pointed out that like Job, John—whose apocalyptic visions were recorded in the last book of the Bible— "saw the fierce and terrible side of Yahweh." For this reason, Jung said, John felt that his gospel of love was one-sided and supplemented it with the gospel of fear: "God can be loved but must be feared," for, "he who loves God will know God." Jung interpreted this as "the eternal, as distinct from the temporal, gospel: *one can love God but must fear him.*"[31] He reasoned that, since the Apocalypse, we know again that God is not only to be loved, but also to be feared, because of the uniting of his antinomies [contradictions].[32]

---

[30] *Answer to Job* (1954): pp. 69, 76, 79; and CW 11: ¶ 640, 648, 651.
[31] *Answer to Job* (1954): pp. 145–146; and CW 11: ¶ 732–733.
[32] *Answer to Job* (1954): pp. 63–64; and CW 11: ¶ 747.

• • •

Jung dealt in *Job* not only with the metaphysical aspects of Yahweh/God and Satan as projections from a human standpoint, but he also brought in the psychological significance of Sophia, citing writings in the Bible (Proverbs), in the apocryphal books (The Wisdom of Solomon; The Wisdom of Jesus the Son of Sirach, or Ecclesiasticus). He commented that Yahweh had lost sight of the "pleromatic existence with Sophia since the dawn of creation," i.e., fullness of being of the divine life, that Sophia's coexistence with Yahweh signified perpetual *hieros gamos* (sacred marriage) "from which worlds are begotten and born."

But, Jung wrote, the reappearance of Sophia/Wisdom in Yahweh's thoughts at the time of the conflict between Job and Yahweh signified an immanent, momentous change: God desired to regenerate by becoming a human being, thereby reinforcing needed self-reflection. Jung interpreted that the influence of Sophia "betokened a new creation" which restored Wisdom to Yahweh's earlier primitive level of consciousness, and thereby balanced the negative side of Yahweh as exposed in *Job* with the "bright side, the kind, just, and amiable aspect of their God."[33]

• • •

In his concern about the "personality" of God, viewed from the standpoint of his Christian upbringing in a pastor's home, Jung expressed many times his objections to

---

[33] *Answer to Job* (1954): pp. 52, 54–55; and CW 11: ¶ 620, 623–625.

the characterization of God as *Summum Bonum* [supreme or highest good]. He wrote (in 1953) on the subject that "the uncompromising Christian interpretation of God as *summum bonum* obviously goes against nature." He stated that the power of God not only reveals itself in the realm of the spirit, but also in the fierce "animality of nature," both within and outside human beings.[34]

In *Answer to Job,* Jung wrote that, when one considers Christ's teaching and the doctrines of the Church, which have emphasized "intensity and exclusiveness" with the goodness of the loving Father in heaven, deliverance from fear, *Summum Bonum* and *privatio boni,* one can form a conception of the "incompatibility which the figure of Yahweh presents." He added that it is impossible for a reflective consciousness to believe that God is the *Summum Bonum,* because such a consciousness does not feel delivered from the fear of God.[35] Jung wrote, in one of his last comments (1958) on *Summum Bonum:*

> It is permissible to assume that the *Summum Bonum* is so good, so high, so perfect, but so remote that it is entirely beyond our grasp. But it is equally permissible to assume that the ultimate reality is a being representing all the qualities of its creation: virtue, reason, intelligence, kindness, consciousness *and their opposites;* to our mind a complete paradox.[36]

---

[34] "Alchemical Symbolism in the History of Religion" in *Psychology and Alchemy* (CW 12, 1953; edn. 2, 1968): ¶ 547.

[35] *Answer to Job* (1954): p. 93; and CW 11: ¶ 662.

[36] *Letters,* vol. 2: p. 435 (3 May 1958 letter to Morton T. Kelsey, Episcopal priest, Monrovia, CA).

He explained that the former view cannot explain away the obvious existence of evil and suffering, and that, unless one assumed the existence of a being "who is in the main unconscious," this age-old question is not answered. He added that such a model would explain why human beings gifted with consciousness were created by God and why the creator "sees himself through the eyes of man's consciousness.[37]

4

ACTS OF GOD

Recognizing God

MOVING FROM THE concept of God's personality as the attempt by Christian believers (as well as their Jewish forerunners in the Old Testament) to conceive of God as personal, one would think about what Jung said regarding God's actions in human life. One of Jung's earliest experiences was reported in *Nietzsche's Zarathustra: Notes of the Seminar Given in 1934–1939*, where he commented that the existence of the devil was an exception to the omnipotence of God. He said:

> When I was a boy I asked my father why there was a devil in the world since God was all powerful, but my father said that God had granted the devil a certain time in which to do his work in order to test people. "But," I said, "if a man makes pots and wants to test whether they are good, he doesn't need a devil, he can do it himself." We still have in the Lord's prayer "lead us not into temptation," and one of my daughters said a good God would know better than to lead people into temptation, and I had nothing to say against that."[1]

---

[1] *Nietzsche's Zarathustra*: p. 1041 (lecture of 5 May 1937).

Such ideas pose serious questions as to how God acts. Another episode in Jung's youth occurred as he was admiring the beautiful cathedral in Basel on his way home from school, reflecting on the beautiful world and that "God made all this and sits above it far in the blue sky on a golden throne" when he experienced a choking sensation. He then spent two days and nights of sheer torture troubled by the dilemma of "thinking praises of the Creator of this beautiful world, . . so why should *I* have to think something inconceivably wicked? Where do such things come from?" He considered that God in his omniscience had arranged it so that the first parents would have to sin, and therefore it was God's intention that they should sin. He then concluded that "God had landed me in this fix without my willing it and had left me without any help." He said that he could not yield to the potentially wicked thought before he understood what God's will was, that God was arranging a decisive test for him, and was he capable of obeying God's will.

So, unable to resist any longer, young Jung let the thought come, which envisioned God sitting on the golden throne, high above the world—and from under the throne "an enormous turd falls upon the sparkling new roof and breaks the walls of the cathedral asunder." Thereupon, he felt an enormous relief, because, instead of an expected damnation, "grace had come upon me." As a consequence of this revelation, he rummaged through his father's library, reading whatever he could find on God, doctrines, and spirit.[2]

That episode illustrated Jung's lifelong viewpoint as expressed in letters written in 1959 near the end of his life.

---

[2] *Memories, Dreams, Reflections* (1962): pp. 36–40 (Jung's autobiography).

He wrote that God is an apt name given to all overpowering emotions in his own psychic system, subduing his conscious will and usurping control over himself. He confided:

> This is the name by which I designate all things which cross my wilful path violently and recklessly, all things which upset my subjective views, plans, and intentions and change the course of my life for better or worse.[3]

He also wrote, in 1959:

> The strange force against or for my conscious tendencies is well known to me. So I say, "I know Him." But why should you call this something "God"? I would ask, "Why not?" It has always been called "God." An excellent and very suitable name indeed. Who could say in earnest that his fate and life have been the result of his conscious planning alone? . . . Individuals who believe they are masters of their fate are as a rule the slaves of destiny. . . . I know what I want, but I am doubtful and hesitant whether the Something is of the same opinion or not.[4]

In writing to a Swiss Protestant minister in 1952, Jung commented: "I share your opinion entirely that man lives wholly when, and only when, he is related to God, to that which steps up to him and determines his destiny."[5]

---

[3] *Letters,* vol. 2: p. 525 (5 December 1959 letter to M. Leonard, King's College, Newcastle upon Tyne, England).

[4] *Letters,* vol. 2: p. 523 (16 November 1959 letter to Valentine Brooke, Worthing, Sussex, England).

[5] *Letters,* vol. 2: p. 66 (28 May 1952 letter to Dorothee Hoch, Protestant minister, Basel, Switzerland).

CONTRADICTORY ASPECTS

Following upon Jung's comments regarding his own personal experiences of God's actions, one thinks of his statement that the "acts of God" have decidedly contradictory aspects. Among answers to questions from Philp in 1958, Jung said:

> In dealing with the moral nature of an act of God, we have either to suspend our moral judgment and blindly follow the dictates of this superior will, or we have to judge in a human fashion and call white white and black black! . . . It is too dangerously easy to avoid responsibility by deluding ourselves that our will is the will of God. We can be forcibly overcome by the latter, but if we are not we must use our judgment, and then we are faced with the inexorable fact that humanly speaking some acts of God are good and some bad.[6]

Jung dealt at great length with the actions of God, as reported by the author of the Book of Job, which he analyzed from a psychological perspective. Assuming the personification of God as Yahweh, as in the story of Job, Jung wrote his interpretations, even though he explained later that he was referring to the God-image in the psyche. Yahweh as a "personality," in Jung's interpretation of the Book of Job, watched jealously over his people, Israel, and

---

[6] *Jung and the Problem of Evil* (1958): pp. 246–247; and in CW 18 (*The Symbolic Life: Miscellaneous Writings* as "Jung and Religious Belief"): ¶ 1667.

gave in easily to the insinuations of Satan without a rebuke or disapproval.[7]

In answers to questions submitted to him in 1956, Jung responded to one on the existence of evil: "We have plenty of evidence in the Old Testament that Yahweh is moral and immoral at the same time, and Rabbinic theology is fully aware of this fact. Yahweh behaves very much like an immoral being, though he is a guardian of law and order." Jung goes on to say that he would call such a personality both immoral and moral and that the God of the Old Testament was good and evil, since Yahweh was the creator of Satan as well as of Christ.[8]

Jung also answered that even the God of the New Testament was still irascible and vengeful, considering that, if God the Father were nothing else than loving, Christ's cruel sacrificial death would be superfluous, to which he added, "I would not allow my son to be slaughtered in order to be reconciled to my disobedient children."[9] He cited a Midrash (exposition of Hebrew scriptures) which said that the Shofar (horn used upon sacred festivals) is still sounded on the Day of Atonement "to remind YHWH of his act of injustice towards Abraham (by compelling him to slay Isaac) and to prevent him from repeating it."[10]

In 1940, in his analysis of the psychological meaning of sacrifice, Jung speculated that, "if mankind is the guilty party" (in the crucifixion of Christ), "logic surely demands

---

[7] *Answer to Job* (1954): p. 44; CW 11: ¶ 616.

[8] *Jung and the Problem of Evil* (1958): pp. 19–20; and in CW 18 (*The Symbolic Life: Miscellaneous Writings* as "Jung and Religious Belief"): ¶ 1593.

[9] *Jung and the Problem of Evil* (1958): pp. 19–20; and in CW 18: ¶ 1593.

[10] "Letter to Père Lachat" (William Lachat, Protestant pastor, Neuchatel) in CW 18: ¶ 1551.

that mankind should be punished. But if God takes the punishment on himself, he exculpates mankind . . . it is not mankind that is guilty, but God, which would logically explain why he took the guilt on himself."[11]

• • •

Jung also commented in *Answer to Job* that Yahweh could do all things and permitted himself all things, and could boast of superior power, to which he added that if, at the end of the *Job* episode, the "mood takes him he can play the feudal grand seigneur and generously recompense his bondslave [Job] for the havoc wrought in his wheat fields. 'So you have lost your sons and daughters? No harm done, I will give you new and better ones.'"[12]

Jung speculated that, remembering "we have sketched no more than an anthropomorphic picture," Yahweh regretted having created human beings, although in his omniscience he must have known all along what would happen to them in exercising their consciousness and potential for independence.[13] Then, continuing the Job story and projecting it, Jung theorized that Yahweh experienced a transformation, saying that God at creation revealed himself in Nature and now wanted to be more specific and become man, that God eternally had wanted to become man and for that purpose continually incarnates through the Holy Ghost.[14]

---

[11] "Transformation Symbolism in the Mass" in *The Mysteries: Papers of the Eranos Yearbooks,* vol. 2, (1955): p. 334; CW 11: ¶ 408.

[12] *Answer to Job* (1954): p. 31; and CW 11: ¶ 597.

[13] *Answer to Job* (1954): p. 15; and CW 11: ¶ 574.

[14] *Answer to Job* (1954): pp. 64, 167; and CW 11: ¶ 631, 749.

Jung posed the question in *Answer to Job* of the transformation of Yahweh from fear to love, of the good God and loving father, whereby such cases "like the Job tragedy are apparently no longer to be expected . . . proves [God] benevolent and gracious . . . shows mercy to the sinful and is defined as Love itself." Also, "He has not lost his wrath and can still mete out punishment, but he does it with justice." Jung brought up the subject of the Lord's Prayer: "Lead us not into temptation, but deliver us from evil," in which the cautious petition and warning was considered appropriate by Christ, "to remind his father of his destructive inclinations towards mankind and to beg him to desist from them."[15]

Jung observed that God had equipped human beings with a little consciousness and a corresponding degree of free will, but that God must also know, "that by so doing he leads them into the temptation of falling into a dangerous independence."[16]

In considering the action of God's "speaking," Jung commented, "it goes against the grain with me to think that the metaphysical God is speaking through everyone who quotes the Bible or ventilates his religious opinions."[17] He also considered the question of how free God is to act, stating that according to the teaching of the church, God cannot be free, being limited to the commands of the church so that God is "fettered by the magic rites of the church . . . can't stop giving his grace."[18]

---

[15] *Answer to Job* (1954): p. 78; and CW 11: ¶ 651.

[16] *Answer to Job* (1954): pp. 85–86; and CW 11: ¶ 658.

[17] "Religion and Psychology: A Reply to Martin Buber" in CW 18 (*The Symbolic Life*): ¶ 1511 (originally written as letter to editor of *Merkur,* Stuttgart, May 1952); published in *Spring* 1973: p. 201.

[18] *Nietzsche's Zarathustra*: pp. 1510–1511 (lecture of 1 February 1939).

WILL OF GOD

In relation to the actions of God, Jung considered the "will of God," as quoted earlier in his answer to Philp (see page 6). In answer to other questions, he responded that the "will of God" often contradicts conscious principles, however good they may seem, and that remorse and penitence follow deviation from God's superior will. He also responded that the will of God could be terrible and could isolate one from family and friends. He commented that it is comparatively easy as long as God wants nothing but fulfillment of God's laws, but "what if he wants you to break them, as he may do equally well?" Jung observed that the true servant of God runs great risks, such as the experience of the prophet Hosea who, at "God's command," married a whore, though, "Poor Hosea could believe in the symbolic nature of his awkward marriage." Jung wondered why God had created consciousness and reason and doubt if complete surrender and obedience to God's will is the ultimate premise or reason, concluding that God wants "reflecting beings who at the same time are capable of surrendering themselves to . . . his will, unafraid of the consequences."[19]

• • •

Among Jung's earliest writings on God's will and actions was his lecture on the Trinity in 1940, in his discussion of the creation, where he considered the story of Lucifer

---

[19] *Jung and the Problem of Evil* (1958): pp. 227–232; and in CW 18: ¶ 1627, 1629, 1637.

(Satan) as an "active principle . . . which opposed to God a counter will of its own." And, because God as Creator willed this, he gave human beings power to will otherwise. Jung reasoned that if God had not done so, he would have created nothing but a machine.[20]

When "fate" is opposed to ego, Jung wrote in 1943, it is difficult not to feel a certain "power" in it, whether divine or infernal. The person who submits to fate calls it the will of God, whereas the person who puts up an exhausting fight is more likely to see the devil in it.[21] Human beings confront the question, "Why do bad things happen to good persons." Is the answer that it is "God's will" valid in all situations? For many, that is not a valid answer.

Jung observed in 1945 that, although we speak sometimes of "God's will," we no longer know what we are saying, for in the same breath we say that where there's a will there's a way—meaning that fate can be overcome by the ego-will.[22]

Responding to a letter from an American college student in 1956, Jung wrote, "Psychologically, the 'Will of God' appears in your inner experience in the form of a superior deciding power, to which you may give various names like instinct, fate, unconscious, faith, etc.," whose criterion is always dynamic superiority. He goes on to say that it is something that one cannot know beforehand; it is

---

[20] "A Psychological Approach to the Doctrine of the Trinity," originally 1940 Eranos lecture in *Eranos-Jahrbuch 1940/41*; in *Symbolik des Geistes* (1948); and in CW 11: ¶ 290.

[21] "Introduction to the Religious and Psychological Problems of Alchemy" in *Psychology and Alchemy* (CW 12, 1953; edn. 2 1968): ¶ 36 note.

[22] "The Psychology of the Transference" (originally in German, 1946); in CW 16 (*The Practice of Psychotherapy*, 1954; edn. 2 1966): ¶ 393.

only known after the fact, and is only learned slowly in the course of one's life. He cautioned that, in applying a moral code (which in itself is a commendable thing), "you can prevent even the divine decision, and then you go astray." He advised that one should "try to live as consciously, as conscientiously, and as completely as *possible* and learn who you are and who or what it is that ultimately decides."[23]

Also late in life (1957), he responded to a letter from Aniela Jaffe, his private secretary, who was tormented with an ethical problem. Jung wrote that he was tormented *by* it in the sense that the problem could not be "caught in any formula" (meaning ethics), because, "what we are dealing with here is the living will of God." He went on to say that he found the will of God always confronting him, and, since it was always stronger than his will, he could only make the tiniest bit of corrections "for better or worse."[24]

In considering his statement that human beings are vessels filled with divine conflict, Jung associated the idea of suffering with a condition in which the inner opposites collide violently with one another. Although he reasoned that all opposites are of God and are incarnated in individuals, he hesitated to describe such painful experiences as being "redeemed." Yet, he went on to say, it cannot be denied that the cross, the great symbol of the Christian faith, is an appropriate representation of the "oppositeness" of the central Christian symbol, and that conscious

---

[23] *Letters,* vol. 2: p. 301 (26 May 1956 letter to William McKinney, student at Northwestern University, Evanston, IL).

[24] *Letters,* vol. 2: pp. 379–380 (9 July 1957 letter to Aniela Jaffe, Jung's secretary, as well as Jungian analyst).

recognition of the opposites, "painful though it may be at the moment, does bring with it a definite feeling of deliverance."[25]

God in the Psyche

The psychic experience of God in the human psyche was basic in Jung's view, considering his statement, "It is only through the psyche that we can establish that God acts upon us." This concept pertained not only to experiences that originate in the psyche itself, but also to outer experiences that are processed by the psyche. Jung wrote, in a letter to a Swiss pastor in 1932, that the human psyche is "boundlessly underestimated," as though God spoke to human beings exclusively through radio, newspapers, or sermons. He asserted that God has never spoken except in and through the psyche, and "the psyche understands it and we experience it as something psychic."[26]

Jung wrote in 1935 that, since the conscious mind does not comprehend the depths of the psyche, "even the believing Christian does not know God's hidden ways," leaving the person to decide whether God will work from outside or from within, i.e., through the soul. He commented that the believer should not shrink from such manifestations as "dreams sent by God," and visions which cannot be traced back to any external causes. He added that it is psychologically unthinkable for God to be simply the "wholly other," because a "wholly other" could never be one of the soul's closest intimacies—which

---

[25] *Answer to Job* (1954): p. 89; and CW 11: ¶ 659.
[26] *Letters,* vol 1: p. 98 (15 August 1932 letter to Swiss pastor, Damour).

is precisely what God is, and that "This correspondence is, in psychological terms, the archetype of the God-image."[27]

At the end of his *Answer to Job,* Jung set forth his position:

> It is only through the psyche that we can establish that God acts upon us, but we are unable to distinguish whether these actions emanate from God or from the unconscious. We cannot tell whether God and the unconscious are two different entities. Both are borderline concepts for transcendental contents. But empirically it can be established, with a sufficient degree of probability, that there is in the unconscious an archetype of wholeness which manifests itself spontaneously through dreams, etc., and a tendency, independent of the conscious will, to relate other archetypes to this centre.[28]

Consequently, Jung supposed that it seemed probable that the archetype of wholeness occupies a central position which approximates it to the God-image in the psyche. He pointed out that the similarity of the archetype and the God-image produces a symbolism that has always characterized and expressed the Deity. He added that, strictly speaking, "the God-image does not coincide with the unconscious as such, but with a special content of it, namely the archetype of the self." Empirically, therefore, the self-archetype cannot be distinguished from the God-image.[29]

---

[27] "Introduction to the Religious and Psychological Problems of Alchemy" in *Psychology and Alchemy* (CW 12, 1953; edn. 2, 1968): ¶ 11.

[28] *Answer to Job* (1954): p. 177; and CW 11: ¶ 757.

[29] *Answer to Job* (1954): pp. 177–178; and CW 11: ¶ 757.

Jung called the self the psychological carrier of the God-image, acting as an archetypal image of one's fullest potential as well as the unifying principle that occupies the central position of authority of the personality as a whole. The self urges one to coordinate and mediate the tension of the opposites, but moral decisions are left to the ego. The lifelong interaction of self and ego determines the individuality and the individuation process of a person's life.[30]

Jung remarked in 1952, regarding Buber's criticisms of his writings:

> when opinions about the same subject differ so widely, there is in my view ground for the suspicion that none of them is correct, and that there has been a misunderstanding. Why is so much attention devoted to the question of whether I am a Gnostic or an agnostic? Why is it not simply stated that I am a psychiatrist whose prime concern is to record and interpret his empirical material? . . . My critics have no right to slur over this in order to attack individual statements taken out of context.[31]

Jung replied to Buber that the "reality of the psyche" was his own working hypothesis and that his main activity consisted in collecting factual material in order to describe and explain it. He pointed out that it was especially evident that it was Buber's apparent inability to understand how such an "autonomous psychic content" as the God-image can burst upon the ego and that such a confrontation

---

[30] *A Critical Dictionary of Jungian Analysis* (1986): p. 135.
[31] "Religion and Psychology: A Reply to Martin Buber" in CW 18 (*The Symbolic Life: Miscellaneous Writings*): ¶ 1500; published in *Spring* 1973: pp. 196–197.

produces a "living experience," and that it was not the task of an empirical scientist to establish how far such a psychic event is dependent on and determined by the existence of a metaphysical deity.[32]

Later, in 1960, Jung wrote a letter to an American professor who had a conversation with Buber in which Buber accused Jung of having reduced God to an object. Jung responded that Buber, "having no practical experience in depth psychology, does not know of the *autonomy of complexes*, a most easily observable fact however." He emphasized that God, as an autonomous complex, was a *subject* confronting him. He stated that the "experience of God" is a psychic fact and that he found himself confronted by something within and more or less represented also by external circumstances which proved to be of insurmountable power. Jung's concern was the question of why Buber could not "get into his head that I deal with psychic facts and not with metaphysical assertions.[33]

•   •   •

Earlier, in 1937, Jung had spoken in his Zarathustra seminar that, "God is a psychological fact that happens to people," and that the idea originated with the experience of an awe-inspiring feeling, a psychical experience when one

---

[32] "Religion and Psychology: A Reply to Martin Buber" in CW 18: ¶ 1507.

[33] *Letters,* vol. 2: pp. 571–572 (29 June 1960 letter to Robert C. Smith, Villanova, PA; later professor at Trenton State College, NJ). Autonomous complexes operate within the psyche's unconscious depths. Complexes are fragments of "personality" which have split off because of traumatic influences or incompatible tendencies. Complexes, according to Jung, behave like independent beings with a high degree of autonomy and come entirely within the scope of the normal, interfering with the intentions of a person's will by disturbing consciousness (CW 8: ¶ 202 and 253).

feels overcome. And though one knows that the experience of God is one's own experience, one must always add that it is not fundamentally a "personal" experience; but it is a mystical experience, a "divine experience."[34]

In this connection, Jung wrote in 1950 that his concept of the God-image was not something invented, but an experience that "comes upon man spontaneously" and can therefore alter the state of consciousness.[35] He expressed this somewhat poetically in a letter to a German man in 1951, writing, "God effervesces in you and sets you to the most wondrous speculation."[36]

Jung also spoke, in 1958, of conscience, which, since olden times, had been understood by many people less as a psychological function than as a divine intervention, "the voice of God," and that it is a *psychological truth* that the opinion exists that the voice of conscience is the voice of God. He wrote in an article on a psychological view of conscience that the dictates of conscience were regarded as *vox Dei*, voice of God. He pointed out that such a view poses an extremely delicate problem, because in practice it is very difficult to "indicate the exact point at which the 'right' conscience stops and the 'false' one begins and what the criterion is that divides one from the other." Presumably it is the moral code, but if the voice of conscience is the voice of God, this voice must possess an incomparably higher authority than traditional morality.[37]

---

[34] *Nietzsche's Zarathustra:* p. 1038 (lecture of 5 May 1937).

[35] *Aion: Researches into the Phenomenology of the Self* (CW 9, Part II, 1959; edn. 2, 1968): ¶ 303.

[36] *Letters,* vol. 2: p. 5 (13 February 1951 letter to Heinrich Boltze, Germany).

[37] "A Psychological View of Conscience" in *Civilization in Transition* (CW 10, 1964; edn. 2 1970): ¶ 839–840 [originally in German 1958 in *Studien aus dem C. G. Jung-Institut, VII,* Zurich).

5

OUR PERSONAL RELATIONSHIP WITH GOD

Access to God

AT THE OTHER SIDE OF God-human relationships is the tremendous variety of relationships we human beings have with our concept of God. These relationships can be with God entirely, they can be predominantly transcendent—that is, "out there" —or with God within—that is, "in there"—or as the God-image in the psyche, or as a combination of "outer/inner God." Jung's reminder is that, in any case, the fact is, "It is only through the psyche that we can establish that God acts upon us," which is the *logos* (thought or word) and ruling principle of this study.

ACCESS TO GOD

Among his earliest writings, Jung wrote, "To assert that God is absolute amounts to placing him outside all connection with mankind," and that such a concept would assign to God "no consequence at all," because, "Man cannot affect him or he man." He observed, then, that we can speak of God only as relative to human beings and of us to God.[1]

---

[1] "The Relation of the Ego to the Unconscious" (1928); in *Two Essays on Analytical Psychology* (CW 7, 1953; edn. 2, 1966): ¶ 394 note.

Jung wrote in 1944 in his introduction to the religious and psychological problems of alchemy:

> It may easily happen that a Christian who believes in all the sacred figures is still undeveloped and unchanged in his inmost soul because he has "all God outside" and does not experience him in the soul. His deciding motives, his ruling interests and impulses, do not spring from the sphere of Christianity but from the unconscious and undeveloped psyche, which is as pagan and archaic as ever. . . . His soul is out of key with his external beliefs. . . . Yes, everything is to be found outside—in image and in word, in Church and Bible—but never inside.[2]

He commented that the archaic (ancient or antiquated) gods reign inside in such instances, which he interpreted as the lack of inner correspondence with the outer God-image. In other words, the inner is undeveloped because of a lack of psychological insight, with the resultant sort of paganism (unenlightened). He emphasized that this connection, "this correspondence is, in psychological terms, the archetype of the God-image." He added that too few people have experienced the divine image as the "innermost possession of their own souls."[3]

---

[2] "Introduction to the Religious and Psychological Problems of Alchemy" in *Psychology and Alchemy* (CW 12, 1953; edn.2, 1968): ¶ 11–12.

[3] Jung referred more often to psyche rather than soul when discussing the totality of all psychic processes. And soul in specific usages referred to the self, a unifying principle within the psyche which occupies the central position of authority and the destiny of the indiviual with similarity to the God-image.

In 1956, he wrote that the meaning and purpose of religion lie in the relationship of the individual to God in Christianity, Judaism, and Islam, and to the path of salvation and liberation in Buddhism—that a "creed" is a confession of faith intended chiefly for the world at large, which expresses a definite collective belief, whereas the word "religion" expresses a subjective or personal relationship with "God."[4] Jung sometimes put the word "God" in quotes to indicate that he was dealing with an "anthropomorphic idea whose dynamism and symbolism are filtered through the medium of the unconscious psyche. Anyone who wants to can at least draw near to the source of such experiences, no matter whether he believes in God or not."[5]

In drawing near to God through the unconscious psyche, Jung asserted that, since "all opposites are of God," we must bend to this "burden," and in doing so we find that God's "oppositeness" is incarnated in the psyche, so that we become "vessels filled with divine conflict."[6]

Jung emphasized that it is quite right that the fear of God should be considered the beginning of all wisdom. He spoke of the "much-vaunted goodness, love, and justice of God" that should be recognized as a genuine experience, not as mere propitiation or reconciliation, because God is a coincidence of opposites. Both the fear of God and the love of God are justified.[7] The opposites are the

---

[4] *The Undiscovered Self* (1959): pp. 20–21; and in *Civilization in Transition* (CW 10, 1964; edn.2, 1970): ¶ 507 (originally in German, 1957).

[5] *The Undiscovered Self* (1959): p. 90; and in CW 10: ¶ 566.

[6] *Answer to Job* (1954): p. 89; and CW 11: ¶ 659.

[7] *Answer to Job* (1954): p. 94; and CW 11: ¶ 664.

ineradicable and indispensable precondition of all psychic life, he wrote in 1955.[8]

• • •

Jung speculated in *Answer to Job* that there is opposition between God and human beings in the Christian view, which might well be a Yahwistic legacy from the Old Testament, when "the metaphysical problem consisted solely in Yahweh's relations with his people." This opposition resulted in our always being in danger of being identified with the dark side. However, if we keep that opposition, we arrive at the Christian conclusion that we are the root of all evil. Considering his position that God had incarnated in human beings and that they needed to become conscious of the sort of God-image with which they were confronted, Jung concluded that God acts out of the unconscious, and forces human beings to harmonize the opposing influences to which the mind is exposed from the unconscious. The unconscious wants to flow into consciousness in order to reach the light. And he asserted that, in striving for unity, we may always count on the help of God.[9]

In trying to harmonize the unconscious opposing influences, Jung stated in 1940 that "God becomes manifest in the human act of reflection." Thereby, human consciousness may analyze any accumulation of unconscious acts (such as dreams), which Jung defined as "achievement

---

[8] "The Personification of the Opposites" in *Mysterium Coniunctionis* (CW 14, 1963; edn. 2 1970): ¶ 206 (originally in German, 1955).

[9] *Answer to Job* (1954): pp. 154–155; and CW 11: ¶ 739–740.

of consciousness . . . as the result of prefigurative archetypal processes or—to put it metaphysically—as part of the divine process."[10] He had observed in 1933 that one may assimilate or respond to a "primordial experience of 'God'" by means of interpretation, speculation, or dogma, or else one may deny it. And he cautioned that one may confuse one's own ideas of the dogma of the "good" God and regard them as sacred because they can be traced back a couple of thousand years.[11]

• • •

In choosing to accept or to deny unconscious pressures on consciousness, Jung set forth in the Terry Lectures on psychology and religion at Yale in 1937 that, "We do not *create* 'God,' we *choose* him." He put this statement in the context of "principalities and powers" that are always with us; we have no need to create them even if we could, commenting that, "we seldom find anybody who is not influenced and indeed dominated by desires, habits, impulses, prejudices, resentments, and by every conceivable kind of complex." He added that all these natural facts function exactly like olympian deities "who want to be propitiated, served, feared and worshipped, not only by the individual owner of this assorted pantheon, but by everybody in his vicinity." This meant that there is always something in the

---

[10] "A Psychological Approach to the Doctrine of the Trinity" (originally in German, *Eranos-Jahrbuch 1940/41*; and in *Symbolik des Geistes,* 1948); and in CW 11: ¶ 238.

[11] "Brother Klaus" in *Psychology and Religion: West and East* (CW 11, 1958; edn. 2, 1969): ¶ 480 (originally in German, 1933).

psyche that takes possession and limits or suppresses one's moral freedom, that one does not enjoy masterless freedom. Therefore, Jung said that one needs to *choose* the master one wishes to serve.[12]

In an interview published in the London Daily Mail (1955) as "Men, Women, and God," Jung remarked that human beings "in this dark atomic age of ours" are once more groping for God; and, without knowing it, they are always concerned with God. He explained that what some people call instinct or intuition is nothing other than God, that God is that voice inside which tells what to do and what not to do—in other words, conscience. He went on to say that he makes his patients understand that everything that happens against their will comes from a superior force and, "God is nothing more than that superior force in our life." Therefore, one can experience God every day.[13]

Access to God includes prayer, as Jung described in 1911, as a wish addressed to God, adding that it is "a concentration of libido on the God-image."[14] He described in another place (response in a letter to an Englishman in 1959) that the God-image is the expression of "an underlying *experience of something* which I cannot obtain by intellectual means, i.e., by scientific cognition." In this same

---

[12] All material quoted in this paragraph comes from *Psychology and Religion* (Terry Lectures 1937), CW 11: ¶ 143.

[13] *C. G. Jung Speaking* (1977): pp. 249–250 ("Men, Women, and God" interview for London *Daily Mail*, 1955).

[14] *Symbols of Transformation* (CW 5, 1956; edn. 2, 1974): ¶ 257 (originally in German, 1911–1912; English edn. 1916 as *Psychology of the Unconscious*). Wording changed from "divinity" to "God" and "unconscious complex" to "God-image."

letter, Jung explained his relationship to God as one of "knowing" rather than "believing" as:

> I mean I know of the existence of God-images in general and in particular. I know it is a matter of universal experience and, in so far as I am no exception, I know that I have such experience also, which I call God.[15]

Jung related in his *Memories, Dreams, Reflections,* that, at age 11, the idea of God began to interest him and he took to praying to God, which somehow satisfied him because he could pray without contradictions—not complicated by distrust.[16] He experienced this because it had become increasingly impossible for him "to adopt a positive attitude to Lord Jesus," who had come into his life at a very early age when the drowned bodies that had been swept over the rocks of the Rhine Falls near his father's church were buried in the parish cemetery. His impression of the solemn men wearing long, black frock coats and unusually tall black hats and shiny black boots bringing a black box gave him vague fears. Then he saw that his father, in his clerical gown, was speaking in a resounding voice while women wept, and there were statements that someone was being buried in the hole in the ground, and that "the Lord Jesus had taken them to himself." Those experiences were complicated further by his experience of fear of a Je-

---

[15] *Letters,* vol. 2: p. 522 (16 November 1959 letter to Valentine Brooke, Worthing, Sussex, England).

[16] *Memories, Dreams, Reflections* (1962): p. 27 (Jung's autobiography).

suit with his long black garment and broad hat, as well as his dream at age 3 of a phallic, "man-eater" underground god which he associated with "Lord Jesus."[17] He had heard that God was a "unique being of whom, so I heard, it was impossible to form any correct conception," although, "He was, to be sure, something like a very powerful old man. But to my great satisfaction there was a commandment to the effect that 'Thou shalt not make unto thee any graven image or any likeness of anything.' Therefore one could not deal with him as familiarly as with Lord Jesus, who was no 'secret.'"[18]

CONDUCT

The relationship between an individual and God involves conduct as well as access, as related above. Jung reported in *Memories, Dreams, Reflections* that, as a schoolboy of 15, he experienced two personalities as a result of "being guilty and at the same time wishing to be innocent." One was the outer person, "son of my parents, who went to school and was less intelligent, attentive, hardworking, decent, and clean than many other boys." The other was the inner person who was grown up, "remote from the world of men, but close to nature . . . and above all close to the night, to dreams, and to whatever 'God' worked directly in him." He explained that in the inner person lived the other, "who knew God as a hidden, personal, and at the same time suprapersonal secret," and commented that, at

---

[17] *Memories, Dreams, Reflections* (1962): pp. 9–12.
[18] *Memories, Dreams, Reflections* (1962): p. 27.

the time, he was not conscious in any articulate way of the two personalities. He went on to say that the play and counterplay between the personalities, "which has run through my whole life, has nothing to do with a 'split' or dissociation in the ordinary medical sense. On the contrary, it is played out in every individual." He ascribed the second as having been of prime importance in his life, having always tried "to make room for anything that wanted to come to me from within."[19]

Jung's youthful experience of church gradually became unsatisfactory, he remembered, because he felt that religious precepts were being put in the place of the will of God as a personal experience and that one's duty was to explore daily God's will. He commented, "Nobody could rob me of the conviction that it was enjoined upon me to do what God wanted and not what I wanted," and that often he had the feeling that, "in all decisive matters I was no longer among men, but was alone with God."[20]

• • •

In one of his early writings (1921), Jung, commenting on the relativity of the God-concept (in contrast to the concept of an "absolute" God who is wholly cut off from human beings), said that it implied a reciprocal and essential relation between humanity and God, whereby "man can be understood as a function of God and God as a psychological function of man." From the empirical point of view

---

[19] All material quoted in this paragraph comes from *Memories, Dreams, Reflections* (1962): pp. 44–45.

[20] *Memories, Dreams, Reflections* (1962): pp. 46–48.

of analytical psychology, he said that the God-image in the psyche is characterized by "its absolute ascendancy over the will of the subject, and can therefore bring about or enforce actions and achievements that could never be done by conscious effort." In other words, the unconscious concentrations of *libido* (psychic energy) in the God-image brings about a powerful impetus to action, or an inspiration that goes beyond conscious understanding. This powerful function can be captured and employed for one's well-being, but also for harmful effects, since the God-image contains the opposites.[21]

By considering the nature and function of one's conscience, as mentioned earlier, as a kind of intervention by "the voice of God," Jung wrote in 1958 that this status allows one to trust in divine guidance and follow one's conscience rather than follow conventional morality, "for better or worse." In this connection, he cautioned about the statement in the Lord's Prayer that "we still beseech God not to lead us into temptation," but "this undermines the very trust the believer should have."[22]

Jung also cautioned (in the Terry Lectures of 1937 at Yale); "That psychological fact which is the greatest power in your system is the god, since it is always the overwhelming psychic factor which is called god." This relationship to the most powerful or highest value, whether positive or negative, is voluntary as well as involuntary,

---

[21] *Psychological Types* (1923): p. 243; and in CW 6 (1971): ¶ 412 (originally in German, 1921).

[22] "A Psychological View of Conscience" in *Civilization in Transition* (CW 10, 1964; edn. 2, 1970): ¶ 840 (originally in German, 1958).

which means that one can accept consciously the value by which one is possessed unconsciously.[23]

Jung had written earlier in his work on psychological types (1921) that this God-concept of concentration of the maximum amount of libido, or psychic energy, in a particular complex of ideas is completely different in different people, that the "highest value operative in a human soul is variously located." He mentioned that there are those "whose God is the belly" (Philippians 3:19), and others for whom God is money, science, power, sex, etc. The whole psychology of the individual, at least in its essential aspects, varies according to the localization of the highest "good,". . . such as power or sex. Thereby, one's conduct can be determined by such values.[24]

Jung used the word "God" many times colloquially in his writings and speaking in an ordinary conversational context. For example, in his letters to Freud he wrote, "my holiday starts tomorrow evening, thank God," and "I hope to God you told him." The most frequent of such phrases in Jung's writings were, "God knows," "Thank God," and "for God's sake," and occasional uses were "praise God," "hope to God," "God forbid," "trusting to God," "God help me," and "My God!" These are common in his letters.

In a letter in 1959, Jung commented that, in relation to God, "I remember Him, I evoke Him, whenever I use His name, overcome by anger or by fear, whenever I

---

[23] *Psychology and Religion* (Terry lectures 1937): p. 98; and in CW 11: ¶ 137. The original wording was "god," whereas the wording in *The Collected Works* put the word in quotation marks and capitalized "God."

[24] *Psychological Types* (1923): p. 46; and in CW 6 (1971): ¶ 67.

involuntarily say: 'Oh God.'" He said that it was an appropriate name by which he designated everything which upset his views, plans, and intentions—for better or worse. He called this the power of fate in a positive as well as negative aspect. He explained that its origin was beyond his control, particularly when it approached him in the form of conscience as a *vox Dei* (voice of God) "with which I can even converse and argue." He emphasized that, "Since I *know* of my collision with a superior will in my own psychic system, *I know of God* . . . just as much dwelling in myself as everywhere else."[25]

---

[25] *Letters,* vol. 2: pp. 525–526 (5 December 1959 letter to M. Leonard, King's College, Newcastle upon Tyne, England).

6

GOD AND THE PSYCHE
Choosing or Creating God

FROM AMONG THE MORE
than six thousand references to God in Jung's writings,
this study has selected approximately four hundred in its
attempt not only to highlight the main themes, but also to
present some elaboration on these themes. In a sense,
then, this chapter is a kind of "summary of a summary."

EXISTENCE

Jung's attitude about the existence of God was that the
physical existence of God is an unanswerable question. Attempts to locate God on a golden throne, or any other
physical evidence prove to be useless, even with the most
powerful telescopes. Therefore, attempts to place a metaphysical God somewhere are assigned to theologians and
others who need to believe in a physical being "out
there." The real question, he said, is the existence of God
in the human psyche, and this comes about through the
experience of "knowing" and not by "believing." He
based this on his knowledge of a primordial or fundamental image as an inborn mode of functioning in the psyche,
so that the knowledge of God comes to consciousness
through the unconscious center of the psyche.

Therefore, Jung stated that only human consciousness reveals God as a fact, existing as a God-image in the deep unconscious of the psyche. He asserted that the God-image is an immediate experience, one of the most natural products of our mental life. Existence itself, whether of the universe or of human beings, he wrote, is "one big unfathomable secret." Nevertheless, we can establish psychically, but not physically, that God is a fact.

Jung wrote that, although one cannot prove the physical existence of God, he knew that God-images play a great role in psychology. Because of the existence of the God-image in the psyche, we can experience God every day. He did not take God's existence on belief, but only on what he experienced, by what he *knew*, which eliminated believing. He knew God as dwelling in himself just as much as everywhere else.

In talking of the God-image as a psychic reality, Jung remarked that he did not deny a transcendental reality. However, metaphysical assertions were of no value to him. As a scientist, he was not concerned with the theological question of God's existence. He argued that, within the frame of psychology, "God" is a dynamic image in the psyche, and that is all that psychology is able to determine about God's existence.

ESSENCE

The essence of God, in consideration of Jung's idea and experience of the God-image as operative in the psyche, was a divine paradox to him. He considered that the essential nature of God was incapable of being expressed in words. The concept of permanent being begged the question of how images and metaphors are with regard to a transcendental "object." It is impossible, he said, to demonstrate the reality of God except by images that arise spontaneously, or by statements that have been sanctified by tradition. Many people never have separated psychic images from their unknowable metaphysical background that tradition tries to affirm.

Jung speculated that the fundamental essence of God might be expressed as permanent being, as substance or matter, or as energy. And he also observed that, whether we view the principle or essential character of existence as being, or matter, or energy, or anything else, we have not created anything, but have simply changed a symbol.

God as "being," Jung cautioned, cannot be assumed to be, as theologians do, a metaphysical absolute being. He did speak of a "unity of being," and of "God as pure reality." He commented on the spiritual concept of "being" as expressed in universal being in Eastern philosophies and religion.

Substance or matter as the basic essence of God was discussed in connection with the alchemists who projected God as the highest value into matter. Jung cautioned, however, that matter as *prima materia* (first matter, or sometimes defined as the indeterminate matter which is the material cause of the universe) is not to be understood as God. In considering spirit as the essence of God, he imagined spirit as an immaterial "substance" that is dynamic and moves one as by the wind.

The concept of energy as essence was considered by Jung first in terms of the power-concept that was the earliest form of a concept of God among primitive peoples. He posed the enigma as to whether "energy is God or God is energy"; and commented that he had to recognize naturalistic values as well as spiritual values. The psychic energy of the libido in the psyche, he said, is a force that is divine because it creates the God-image inside by making use of archetypal patterns.

PERSONALITY

In addition to considerations of the existence of God and of the essence of God, Jung wrote at length about the "personality" of God. This involved description and analysis of images of God that human beings hold as to the attributes, characteristics, and qualities of their "God-images," which involved the God "out-there" as well as the God "in-there." He observed that one can assert nothing except that the outside world and the psyche are a reflection of the God that one imagines, which commonly involves a body perceived by the senses and a spirit which is conscious of itself. Consequently, Jung wrote, one is dealing with either God as imagined in human form, or as an indescribable model with human attributes and emotions. He commented that an absolute God (outside connections with human beings) "does not concern us . . , whereas a 'psychological' God would be *real*." And this involves identity and personal characteristics, including persona or the "mask" with which the individual confronts the world, as well as the shadow or the negative side of the personality, the sum of all of the unpleasant qualities one wants to hide, including the inferior, worthless, and primitive side of human nature.

Jung, writing that although God never was invented but was always an occurrence or psychological experience, one is required to say something definite about God because God is an object of worship. This included the attributes from Christian doctrine of omnipresence, omniscience, omnipotence, immutability, eternity, creator and preserver, and morally perfect being. Jung commented on many of such attributes, such as God as immovable or as evolving, but not in a systematic way.

In response to the problem of Job, Jung examined the paradox or contradictory God-image in the unity or one-ness of God, which posed the existence of opposites in the immense energy of the Deity. He listed some of the antinomies (contradictory principles) of opposites in God's "personality" in the Book of Job, which were: God is immovable, *yet* a stimulator of motion; eternal source as well as goal; creator of growth *and* decay; supreme light as well as abysmal darkness; and infinite as well as finite in personality.

Jung's view of the existence of opposites in God/Yahweh was dramatically presented in his *Answer to Job*, which resulted from the climax of a lifetime of questions about God. His analysis of the God-image which had been projected onto Yahweh as a personality by the writer(s) of the Book of Job resulted in a great deal of criticism, especially from theologians. Although late in his long life (1959), he wrote that the book did not refer to "God himself," but that it represented the "opinion man makes of God," his use of language in Job posed a problem. His claim that he always meant "God-image" when he spoke of "God" is difficult to reconcile in view of the fact that the word "God-image" was used only eleven times in *Answer to Job*, whereas "God" appeared nearly 400 times and "Yahweh" about 160 times. Another difficulty is that he used both "God" and "Yahweh" on most pages of his book, frequently in the same paragraph and occasionally in the same sentence, which posed the question of what the reader experiences as possibly anthropomorphic images, such as those experienced by the writer of the Book of Job.

Jung commented that the Book of Job demonstrated "the absence of human morality in Yahweh is a stumbling block." He dealt with Yahweh's behavior primarily from the point of view of morality, justice and injustice, fear and love, which put human beings in an impossible position in trying to adjust to such a paradoxical nature of God.

In *Answer to Job,* Jung's thesis was that Yahweh's powerful personality demonstrated a lack of reflective consciousness in Yahweh's treatment of Job. With the reappearance of Sophia as Wisdom in the Job episode, Jung wrote, there came a rise in Yahweh's consciousness, which brought about a change.

In analyzing the Job story from the point of view of Yahweh's "personality," Jung questioned the testing of Job's faithfulness and the consequences of Yahweh's "bet with Satan." He pondered the possibility that Yahweh had some secret resistance against Job, possibly that Job as a human being had something that Yahweh did not have, such as a somewhat keener consciousness. What would explain the suffering—Job's loss of children, all property, and wretched sickness? Jung considered that when the "divine wager" with Satan came to an end suddenly with Yahweh's "impressive performance" of power, Job shrewdly acceded to the reality of that power, realizing that his questions had not been answered and that Yahweh could not be called to account because "morality presupposes consciousness."

Jung concluded that Job had recognized Yahweh's contradictory nature, so that Yahweh must become "man" because Yahweh had wronged Job—that, in a sense, Job had surpassed Yahweh in consciousness; therefore, Yahweh must be regenerated by incarnating in humanity, specifically in Christ, and must suffer consciously those opposites within. He brought in the psychological significance of Sophia and her coexistence with Yahweh, whose reappearance in Yahweh's thoughts signified a momentous change by considering the need for self-reflection.

Jung also brought up the terrible double aspect of God in his analysis of the Biblical Revelation of John (Apocalypse) by contrasting John's one-sided gospel of God as love with God's judgment and punishment in the Apocalypse. This, Jung said, supplemented the Christian gospel of love with a gospel of fear, so that God *can* be loved but *must* be feared because of the union of opposites in the God-image in the human psyche. Jung added that human beings, created by God and gifted with consciousness, explained the situation that the Creator "sees himself through the eyes of man's consciousness."

ACTS OF GOD

Jung recalled that his personal experience of the actions of God occurred very early in his life, among which was his "temptation" to yield to a potentially "wicked" thought as he contemplated God sitting on a golden throne high in the beautiful blue sky above the sparkling cathedral in

Basel, commenting that "the world is beautiful." He choked and then wrestled for two days and nights with the potential thought and finally concluded that God had arranged a decisive test of "obeying God's will." He reasoned that God "in his omniscience had arranged it so that the first parents would have to sin"; therefore, it was God's will in testing him so that he could experience grace.

This episode illustrated Jung's lifelong viewpoint that one lives wholly only when one is related to God, to that which steps up to him and determines his destiny. He wrote that "God" meant everything that crossed his path and that upset his subjective views, plans, intentions, and changed "the course of my life for better or worse."

Considering the contradictory aspects of the energies within the divine source, Jung stated that, from the human point of view, "some acts of God are good and some bad." He dealt at great length with the actions of God in the Book of Job, analyzing from a psychological perspective the personification of God as Yahweh, citing Yahweh's giving in to testing the faithfulness of Job at the insinuations of Satan and behaving like an immoral being according to human expectations. He considered that the God of the New Testament, though characterized as all-loving, was still vengeful, citing the cruel, sacrificial death of Christ as superfluous, adding that Jung himself would not allow his own son to be killed "in order to be reconciled to his disobedient children." He speculated in his study of the meaning of Christ's sacrifice that "mankind should be punished" in the crucifixion "if mankind is the guilty party," but if God takes the punishment, "God took the guilt on himself."

In *Answer to Job,* Jung described Yahweh as capable of doing all things, boasting of superior power over everything, but in the end Yahweh reflected upon the treatment of Job and wanted to experience a transformation by a special incarnation in humanity. He posed the question of the transformation of Yahweh from fear to love, the good God and loving Father. However, he mentioned that the petition in the Lord's Prayer to "lead us not into temptation" was a caution from Christ to remind his Father, God, of destructive inclinations. Jung observed that God, having provided human beings with some consciousness and free will, must know that in so doing, "he leads them into the temptation of falling into a dangerous independence."

WILL OF GOD

As an aspect of the acts of God, Jung wrote that the "will of God" could be terrible as well as good, citing the awkward marriage of the prophet Hosea, who obeyed "God's command" to marry a prostitute. Jung pondered why God had created human reason if complete obedience to God's will is the final premise. He reasoned that, considering the story of Satan at Creation as a counter-will opposed to God, human beings received power to will otherwise. He also observed that one may speak of God's will, but at the same time say that "where there's a will there's a way"—that fate can be overcome by ego-will.

Commenting on the will of God as a superior deciding power in one's life, Jung advised that one should try to live as consciously and conscientiously as possible in order to learn who one is and who or what ultimately decides. He also said that the problem could not be solved by ethics, because one is dealing with the "living will of God," and that he, himself, found the will of God always confronting him. Therefore, he could only make "the tiniest bit of correction for better or worse" in God's always stronger will. He considered that it is comparatively easy to obey God's "laws"; but what happens when "God's will" wants one to break them?

GOD IN THE PSYCHE

Jung's statement: "It is only through the psyche that we can establish that God acts upon us," is basic in his analysis of the actions of God, that God has never spoken except in and through one's psyche, whether it be experiences that originate within the psyche or outer experiences that must be processed by the psyche. Since the conscious mind has difficulty understanding the unconscious processes in the psyche, he commented that one should not shrink from visions and "dreams sent by God," because God is not "wholly other," but has correspondence to the archetype of the God-image in the depths of the psyche from which to "act." And thereby God may operate independent of one's conscious will, though the ego may or may not assert its own will.

Jung wrote that the God-image was not something invented, but was an experience that comes spontaneously and can alter the state of consciousness. He said that, empirically, the archetype of the Self cannot be distinguished from the God-image. The Self may be called the carrier of the God-image that occupies the central position of authority of the personality as a whole and that it can burst upon the ego, producing a "living experience." He also said that the experience of God is not basically a "personal" experience, but is a mystical, "divine experience."

In speaking of conscience, Jung wrote that the idea of conscience being the "voice of God" posed a delicate problem because of the difficulty of knowing the point at which the "right" conscience stops and the "false" one begins. He said that if the voice of conscience is the voice of God, it must have a higher authority than traditional moral codes.

OUR RELATIONSHIPS WITH GOD

The relationship of the individual to God is tremendously varied in relation to his or her concept of God, particularly in response to a presumption that God is entirely or mostly transcendent ("out there"), or that God is predominantly within ("in there") as the God-image in the psyche, according to Jung's view. Various combinations of inner/ outer occur. Jung reminds us that the ruling principle is that "it is only through the psyche that we can establish that God acts upon us"—whether or not the experience is prompted by an outside source.

Access to God as viewed always from "outside" through sacred objects (images and words in Church and Bible), Jung wrote, tends to leave a Christian undeveloped "in his inmost soul," because of a lack of psychological consciousness. He added that too few individuals experience the divine image as "the innermost possession of their own souls" for lack of correspondence between the outer image of God and the inner God-image. By drawing near to God through the unconscious psyche where "all opposites are of God," Jung observed that the individual must adapt to the God-image in order to experience the beginning of wisdom, which is the fear of God and the love of God.

In adapting to the God-image in the sense that God acts out of the unconscious with its opposing influences. Jung commented that the unconscious wants to flow into consciousness so that it might reach the light and that one must harmonize the psychic energies. In striving for unity, he asserted that one may always count on God's help, stating: "God becomes manifest in the human act of reflection," whereby one's ego consciousness may analyze unconscious acts, such as dreams, in order to have access to God. He observed that one may respond to God by means of interpretation, speculation, or dogma, or even deny the experience of the God-image.

Jung emphasized that "we do not *create* 'God,' we *choose* him," by accepting or denying the God-image's pressures from the unconscious. He stated that there is always something in the psyche that takes possession and limits one's moral freedom, often dominating by desire, impulse, prejudice, resentment, and by "every conceivable kind of complex." He observed that human beings "in this dark atomic age of ours" are always concerned with God, though groping and not knowing what the access to God might be. He added that one can experience God every day.

Access to God, Jung explained, includes prayer (a wish addressed to God), which is a "concentration of libido on the God-image," not attainable by intellectual means, but by a kind of "knowing" rather than "believing." He took to praying to God when he was 11, he said, in contrast to his praying to the "Lord Jesus" as a young child.

Jung wrote that one's relationship to God involves conduct as well as access. He said that, instead of putting religious (meaning church) precepts in place of the will of God as a personal experience, one should explore God's will daily. He commented that the reciprocal relationship between human beings and God should be that a person is a "function of God and God is a psychological function of man." He added that the God-image can bring about a powerful impetus to action or inspiration that could never be done by conscious effort. However, one needs to remember that, because the God-image contains opposites, this powerful function can be used for one's well-being, or even for harmful effects.

With regard to divine guidance, Jung observed that one needs to follow one's conscience rather than conventional morality "for better or worse," though the distinction between a good and a false conscience is sometimes difficult. He remarked that one's conduct can be determined by such values as money, power, sex, science, etc., which, when operating as the highest value in a person's life is that person's "god," replacing the "God" which the person "claims" to be the real one, particularly in public statements.

EPILOGUE

AUTHOR'S VIEW ON JUNG AND GOD

In attempting to present these highlights of Jung's thoughts about God, I am aware of the problems that such an attempt entails. In addition to the fact that, in such a relatively brief presentation, my intuitive selection of about four hundred of the more than six thousand references to God, I may have inserted some of my own interpretations of Jung's thoughts. My intention has been to be as faithful as possible to Jung's own voice, including quotations, in order to be able to give the "flavor" of his wording.

At this time I want to give some of my own impressions about Jung's views of God. I agree with most of his ideas, especially his insistence upon the viewpoint that the matter of the existence of God comes from *knowing* rather than *believing*. In my early Christian life I resisted the injunction that one needs "only" to believe to be saved, realizing that, for me, an acceptance of someone else's pressure to believe as he or she does is questionable. This approach seemed to leave out the necessity of my seeking knowledge and gnosis, or insight (deep wisdom). During my youth I heard our well-known Methodist missionary to India, E. Stanley Jones, say that "the kingdom of God is within." This statement impressed me greatly and has stayed with me. In my later years, through depth psychology, that idea has been expanded to include "the kingdom of Hell is within" also.

During my teen years I questioned the literalness of the Bible and its preaching. It was as though I had become *myself* and could *will,* whereas before I had been willed to do this and that. Most importantly, I sought the meaning behind the dogma and miracles, though I admitted that miracles are certainly possible and do occur. I read the Bible completely from cover to cover and repeated the exercise more than once in the years to come, highlighting the Scriptures for significant or questionable writing.

With regard to the existence of God, I agree with Jung that the concept of God as a physical being is a question that cannot be answered. And the theological views of God's existence are unsatisfying. If questioned, as was Jung, whether I "believed" in God when I was a child, which perforce conjured up an oversized, impressive old man with a long white beard sitting on a golden throne in the beautiful heavens and presenting a kind as well as stern manner, I would have said, "Yes." But in later life I considered this metaphysical view to be untenable. I have come to think that, if one needs to "personify" God in order to grasp the "inconceivable" other, the best symbol for the original unity of God is a oneness of gender, that is, Father-Mother or Mother-Father in one—impossible to know which came first, or if there were a "first."

As a scientist, I am unable to discover a physical, transcendent being out there in the universe and maybe not even beyond the universe, if the universe were to have boundaries. I tend to accept a Gnostic idea from the Gospel of Philip, in answer to the question, "What is outside of the outer?" The answer: "The lord called the outer darkness 'destruction,' and there is nothing outside of it."

In other words, whatever I imagine the outer darkness to hold, destruction immediately destroys it.

Nevertheless, I know of an awe-inspiring spirit within my psyche, and I am satisfied that this represents a divine God-image that came into my being in this life from an indefinable, original source far back in my genetic history. In that sense, God is *real*.

I consider that wholeness or unity was the original condition of existence, before the first "thought" came forth from the "mind" of God and began to discriminate "this" from "that." From among Jung's speculations on the essential nature of God, the energy-concept of the essence of God resonates with my need for symbols. The psychic energy of libido as a force in my psyche, it seems to me, represents a "mini" image in me that is a vital impetus from God. And, connected with this is the opinion that I regard the spirit of God as a dynamic *substance* in the sense that such "immaterial" substances as light and wind are real and reach us. I agree that it is impossible to find God outside the human psyche, whether as a metaphysical "body, "energy," or "spirit," and that, ultimately, I only know of God "within" myself because my psychic "mind-body" has to process all outer and inner sensations or perceptions. Consequently, my view is that the God-image within represents the design or psychic device which informs me of "that of God."

My opinion, in line with Jung, is that the attributes of God, as viewed from a human perspective, encompass all opposites; otherwise, there would not be unity in the All, the monotheistic, only true God. Therefore, the unconscious depths of my psyche teem with the interplay of opposites with their powerful energies, which are fundamentally based upon instincts, including the instinct of spirituality—all of which propel their energies to become represented as archetypes (structuring patterns) that manifest images, of either positive or negative energy that may be perceived by consciousness by means of dreams or visions. An archetype, then, links instinct and images, as well as body and psyche.

With regard to the concept of the personality of God, i.e., the characteristics and attributes ascribed to God, I realize that this comes from a recognition that we are constrained (because of our humanity) to view God as similar to us, though vastly greater.

I have difficulty with Jung's idea that God, or more specifically the Yahweh of the Old Testament, had a rather dim consciousness. This comes into play particularly as I interpret Jung's *Answer to Job* in my regard that the "poet-author" of the Book of Job in the Bible projected a simplistic view of Yahweh that reflected a psychological condition of authoritarian power over the Israelites who were being tested for faithful obedience. Job eventually acceded to that power, even though he thought he had not received a "fair trial." If one were to substitute the word "God-image" for Yahweh, one would recognize that the prevailing image in the psyches of the Israelites was a mostly negative power-complex, which does not mean that "God" was/is like that.

I doubt Jung's interpretation that, as a result of Yahweh's reflection on the matter, he decided to undergo incarnation in Jesus as Christ. My view is that God has incarnated and continues to incarnate in everyone, and that the Christ-archetype in Jesus is the perfect symbol of the hidden immortal within mortal human beings, a bringing together of God and humanity within each of us.

In considering the actions of God as reported in the Bible and as experienced in individual lives, I tend to agree with Jung that God meant everything which crossed his path and upset his own views, plans, and intentions and changed the course of his life for better or worse. I agree with his comments on the will of God and with his statements on conscience, including the voice of God, which has a higher authority than traditional morality.

Jung's most extensive comments on the actions of God are evident in his book *Answer to Job*. His hypothesis that the Job episode resulted in the transformation of God from the fearful Yahweh of the Old Testament into the God of love in the New Testament represents to me a transformation of projections by the "writers" of the Scriptures as representative of the "beliefs" of their people. This view was overly simplified, I think, because the Old Testament God was considered to have also mercy and compassion and the New Testament God to have punishment with justice. Jung presented very well, in the case of the disciple John, who experienced both God in Christ as love in his gospel, and God as destroyer in Revelation, that God as the unity of opposites can be loved and also must be feared, as the beginning of Wisdom.

The main stumbling-block in Jung's thesis, in my opinion, was his trying to analyze God as represented by the anthropomorphic figure of Yahweh, though a few years later he stated that, in his book, he did not refer to God "himself," but rather to the opinion or idea one has of God. In view of Jung's recognition of the existence of opposites in God, I agree with his emphasis that "God can be loved but must be feared," a reflection, it seems to me, of the essential differences in emphasis between the Old and New Testaments.

Since I have difficulty ascribing metaphysically a personality of a transcendent God "out there," I can imagine, however, that, whatever the source, there are attributes and qualities of God that are somehow incarnated in my own life. I tend to think that the source and channel of God's actions are etherial energy, encompassed in light, whose power is manifested in spiritual energy in my life by means of "actions of God" coming from the depths of my unconscious. My own nature as a "sensate type," and my training and experience as a scientist prompt me to seek physical answers, so that I have a strong need to put everything in space and time, and to establish a structure to everything, including the psyche; realizing, however, that there is a multitude of intangibles in life that also must be accepted as reality.

In trying to envision the process of God in my life, I visualize that sparks of divine light fall upon the created world and find refuge in the hidden recesses of my psyche/soul. The heat of the light shocks me into awareness of the sparks in me. God provides a "messenger," whom I call the God-image, to stand guard over me until the spark begins to glow as inner wisdom.

Jung's emphasis on the concept that we do not create God, but that we choose God by accepting or denying the pressures from the unconscious, resonates with my experience. My consciousness can analyze unconscious actions, such as dreams viewed as the "voice of God," or psychic outbursts, in order to have access to God; and, in striving for unity, as Jung said, I may count on God's help. I agree that one can experience God every day and that prayer and a good rather than a false conscience, though sometimes difficult to distinguish, are essential for seeking "God's will."

I call upon my own internal voice, which is linked with the universal voice of God, for gnosis (inner knowing).

I also agree, wholeheartedly, with his observation that the highest value in a person's life, whether it be power, money, sex, or any other overwhelming drive, is that person's "god," no matter what may be the "claim" that the God of truth, or the "God in heaven" is that person's real guide. It seems to me that those (of us all) who claim allegiance to the God of Truth need to examine the "bottom line" for what fundamentally controls our lives.

Finally, from my experience of prayer, in the context of personal prayer, as well as communal prayer (in the traditional Quaker meeting for worship of God in silence until one may be led by the Spirit to share insights), I have not outgrown the need for the classic meditative prayer of praise, thanksgiving, confession, intercession, and petition to the *transcendent* God. However, I also search the depths to experience the practice of contemplative prayer to the *immanent* God-(image), beyond words and thinking.

CHRONOLOGY OF JUNG'S WRITINGS ON GOD

Dates refer to completion of writing or lecture, wherever known, not date of publication, whether in German, English, or French; *CW* refers to volume and number of item in *The Collected Works of C. G. Jung.*

Jung's Writings on God

Year	Age	Work
1878	3	*Memories, Dreams, Reflections:* pp. 13–19
1886	11	*Memories, Dreams, Reflections:* p. 27
1887	12	*Memories, Dreams, Reflections:* pp. 36–43
?		*Zarathustra* seminar: pp. 1041, 1369
1890	15	*Memories, Dreams, Reflections:* pp. 45–48, 54–56
1891?	16	*Memories, Dreams, Reflections:* pp. 56–63
1891–1892	16–17	*Memories, Dreams, Reflections:* pp. 67–69
1893–1895	18–20	*Memories, Dreams, Reflections:* pp. 91–96
1897?	22	*Memories, Dreams, Reflections:* pp. 97–98
		Zofingia lecture: pp. 23, 46
1899	24	*Zofingia* lecture: pp. 102–108
1905	30	*CW* 18:4 [Spiritualistic Phenomena]
1907	32	*The Freud/Jung Letters:* pp. 44, 92
1908	33	*The Freud/Jung Letters:* pp. 163, 170
1908–1909?		*Memories, Dreams, Reflections:* pp. 126, 139–140
1909	34	*The Freud/Jung Letters:* p. 261

Jung's Writings on God (continued)

Year	Age	Work
1909	34	*CW* 4:14 [The Significance of the Father in the Destiny of the Individual]
1909–1910?		*Memories, Dreams, Reflections:* pp. 151, 168, 201
1910	35	*The Freud/Jung Letters:* pp. 294, 308, 325, 375
		CW 17:1 [Psychic Conflicts in a Child]
1911–1912	36	*CW* 5 [Wandlungen und Symbole der Libido; 1916 English: Psychology of the Unconscious]
1912	37	*CW* 7:3 [New Paths in Psychology]
		The Freud/Jung Letters: p. 532
		C. G. Jung Speaking [America Facing its Most Tragic Moment]
1914	39	*CW* 3:3 [On Psychological Understanding]
1915	40	*Letters:* vol. 2, p.31
1916	41	*Memories, Dreams, Reflections:* Appendix V [Seven Sermons to the Dead]
		CW 8:9 [The Psychology of Dreams]
		CW 18:35 [Adaptation, Individuation, Collectivity]
1917	42	*CW* 7:1-2 [Psychology of Unconscious Processes]
1918	43	*CW* 10:1 [The Role of the Unconscious]
1919	44	*CW* 3:6 [On the Problem of Psychogenesis in Mental Diseases]
1921	46	*CW* 6 [Psychologische Typen; 1923 English: Psychological Types]

Jung's Writings on God (continued)

Year	Age	Work
1922	47	C. G. *Jung Speaking* [Esther Harding's Notebooks]
1923	48	*CW* 17:3 [Child Development and Education]
		Letters: vol. 1, pp. 40–41
1924	49	*CW* 10:5 [The Love Problem of a Student]
1925	50	*CW* 17:8 [Marriage as a Psychological Relationship]
		Analytical Psychology [seminar notes]
		Memories, Dreams, Reflections: p. 253
1926	51	*Memories, Dreams, Reflections*: pp. 156 157, 267, 269
		CW 8:12 [Spirit and Life]
		Letters: vol. 1, p. 44
1927	52	*CW* 8:14 [Analytical Psychology and Westanschauung]
		CW 10:2 [Mind and Earth]
		CW 10:5 [Woman in Europe]
1928	53	*CW* 8:1 [Psychic Energy]
		CW 8:7 [The Structure of the Psyche]
		CW 10:4 [The Spiritual Problem of Modern Man]
		CW 11:8 [Psychoanalysis and the Cure of Souls]
		Letters: vol. 1, p. 51
		Dream Analysis [seminar notes]
1929	54	*Dream Analysis* [seminar notes]
		CW 4:16 [Freud and Jung: Contrasts]

Jung's Writings on God (continued)

Year	Age	Work
1930	55	*CW* 13:1 [Commentary on "The Secret of the Golden Flower"] *CW* 15:1 [Paracelsus] *Letters*: vol. 1, p. 57, 58, 61–62, 65 *CW* 4:15 [Introduction to Kranefeldt's Secret Ways of the Mind] *CW* 10:3 [Archaic Man] *CW* 10:20 [The Rise of a New World] *CW* 10:22 [The Complications of American Psychology] *CW* 15:5 [Richard Wilhem: In Memorium] *CW* 15:7 [Psychology and Literature] *Letters*: vol. 1, p. 75 *Dream Analysis* [seminar notes] *Visions* [seminar notes]
1931	56	*Visions* [seminar notes] *CW* 8:13 [Basic Postulates of Analytical Psychology] *CW* 10:7 [The Meaning of Psychology for Modern Man]
1932	57	*CW* 11:7 [Psychotherapists or the Clergy] *CW* 15:3 [Sigmund Freud in His Historical Setting] *CW* 15:8 ["Ulysses": A Monologue] *CW* 17:7 [The Development of Personality] *Letters*: vol. 1, pp. 91, 98, 107 *Visions* [seminar notes]

Jung's Writings on God (continued)

Year	Age	Work
1933	58	*Visions* [seminar notes]
		CW 9.i:11 [A Study in the Process of Individuation]
		CW 11:6 [Brother Klaus]
		Letters: vol. 1, pp. 123, 124–125
1934	59	*CW* 9.i:1 [Archetypes of the Collective Unconscious]
		CW 10:21 [La Révolution Mondiale]
		CW 10:26 [A Rejoinder to Dr. Bally]
		C. G. Jung Speaking [Does the World Stand on the Verge of Spiritual Rebirth?]
		Visions [seminar notes]
		Nietzsche's Zarathustra [seminar notes]
1935	60	*Nietzsche's Zarathustra* [seminar notes]
		CW 11:11 [Psychological Commentary on The Tibetan Book of the Dead]
		CW 12:3 [Dream Symbolism in Alchemy]
		CW 16:1 [Principles of Practical Psychotherapy]
		CW 16:3 [What is Psychotherapy?]
		CW 18:1 [Analytical Psychology: Theory and Practice]
		Letters: vol. 1, pp. 195–196, 202
1936	61	*Letters*: vol. 1, pp. 213, 216
		CW 9.i:2 [The Concept of the Collective Unconscious]
		CW 9.i:3 [Concerning the Archetypes]
		CW 10:10 [Wotan]

Jung's Writings on God *(continued)*

Year	Age	Work
		CW 11:12 [Yoga and the West]
		CW 12:3 [Religious Ideas in Alchemy]
		CW 18:70 [Psychology and National Problems]
		CW 18:126 [On the "Rosarium Philosophorum"]
		Nietzsche's Zarathustra [seminar notes]
1937	62	*Nietzsche's Zarathustra* [seminar notes]
		CW 11:1 [Psychology and Religion]
		CW 13:2 [The Visions of Zosimos]
		C. G. Jung Speaking [Is Analytic Psychology a Religion?]
1938	63	*CW* 9.i:4 [Psychological Aspects of the Mother Archetype]
		CW 18:5 [Occult Phenomena]
		CW 18:116 [Foreword to Gilli's "Der dunkle Bruder"]
		Nietzsche's Zarathustra [seminar notes]
1939	64	*Nietzsche's Zarathustra* [seminar notes]
		CW 9.i:5 [The Different Aspects of Rebirth]
		CW 10:23 [The Dreamlike World of India]
		CW 11:10 [Psychological Commentary on The Tibetan Book of the Great Liberation]
		CW 11:13 [Foreword to Suzuki's *Introduction to Zen Buddhism*]

Jung's Writings on God (continued)

Year	Age	Work
1940	65	*CW* 15:4 [In Memory of Sigmund Freud] *CW* 18:3 [The Symbolic Life] *Letters*: vol. 1, pp. 262-263 *CW* 9.i:6 [Psychology of the Child Archetype] *CW* 11:2 [A Psychological Approach to the Dogma of the Trinity]
1941	66	*CW* 11:3 [Transformation Symbolism in the Mass] *CW* 15:2 [Paracelsus the Physician] *CW* 16:6 [Psychotherapy and a Philosophy of Life] *CW* 16:8 [Psychotherapy Today] *Letters*: vol. 1, pp. 293, 294, 296
1942	67	*CW* 13:3 [Paracelsus as a Spiritual Phenomenon] *CW* 13:4 [The Spirit Mercurius] *CW* 16:7 [Psychotherapy and a Philosophy of Life] *CW* 17:5 [The Gifted Child]
1943	68	*CW* 18:131 [Depth Psychology and Self-Knowledge] *Letters*: vol. 1, pp. 332–333, 336–337, 338, 340 *Letters*: vol. 2, p. xxxvi
1944	69	*Letters*: vol. 1, pp. 345, 348–350 *CW* 11:15 [The Holy Men of India]

Jung's Writings on God (continued)

Year	Age	Work
1945	70	*CW* 12:3,I [Introduction to Religious and Psychological Problems of Alchemy]
		CW 9.i:8 [The Phenomenology of the Spirit in Fairytales]
		CW 10:11 [After the Catastrophe]
		CW 13:5 [The Philosophical Tree]
		CW 16:13 [The Psychology of the Transference]
		CW 18:73 [Marginalia on Contemporary Events]
		C. G. Jung Speaking [The Post-War Psychic Problems of the Germans]
		C. G. Jung Speaking [Allenby's Contact with Jung]
		Letters: vol. 1, pp. 360–361, 364–365, 368, 372–373, 384–387, 392, 395–396, 399–400
1946	71	*CW* 8:8 [On the Nature of the Psyche]
		CW 10:13 [Essays on Contemporary Events]
		Letters: vol. 1, pp. 408–412, 450
1947	72	*Letters:* vol. 1, pp. xxxix, 466, 474, 480
		C. G. Jung Speaking [A Visit from a Young Quaker]
1948	73	*C. G. Jung Speaking* [A Visit from Alberto Moravia]

Jung's Writings on God (continued)

Year	Age	Work
1949	74	*Letters*: vol. 1, pp. 284–286, 486–488, 492, 506 *Letters*: vol. 1, pp. 536, 540 *CW* 11:16 [Foreword to the *I Ching*] *CW* 18:54 [Foreword to Neumann's *The Origin and History of Consciousness*]
1950	75	*CW* 8:18 [Synchronicity] *CW* 9.i:12 [Concerning Mandala Symbolism] *CW* 18:93 [Foreword to Allenby's *A Psychological Study of the Origins of Monotheism*] *C. G. Jung Speaking* [Kenneth Lambert's Contact with Jung] *C. G. Jung Speaking* [Man and His Environment] *Letters*: vol. 1, p. 556
1951	76	*Letters*: vol. 2, pp. 4–5, 6–9, 9, 14, 16, 21–23, 28–29 *CW* 9.ii [Aion] *CW* 11:5 [Foreword to Werblowsky's *Lucifer and Prometheus*]
1952	77	*CW* 11:4 [Foreword to White's *God and the Unconscious*] *CW* 11:9 [Answer to Job] *CW* 18:96 [Religion and Psychology: A Reply to Martin Buber]

Jung's Writings on God (continued)

Year	Age	Work
		Letters: vol. 2, pp. 32–34, 39, 50, 52–53, 54, 60–61, 62, 64–65, 65–68, 70–71, 72–73, 74–78, 85–86, 86–87, 88–89
		C. G. Jung Speaking [Eliade's Interview]
1953	78	*CW* 18:98 [Letters to Pere Bruno]
		Letters: vol. 2, pp. 102, 110, 112, 118, 120, 122–123, 129– 130, 134–138, 141–142, 145
1954	79	*Letters:* vol. 2, pp. 147, 152–154, 154–155, 165–170, 198–199
		CW 9.i:9 [On the Psychology of the Trickster-Figure]
		CW 14 [Mysterium Coniunctionis]
		CW 18:99 [Letter to Père Lachat]
		CW 18:100 [On Resurrection]
1955	80	*CW* 9.i:13 [Mandalas]
		C. G. Jung Speaking [Men, Women, and God]
		C. G. Jung Speaking [An Eightieth Birthday Interview]
		Letters: vol. 2, pp. 205–207, 209, 235–238, 239–242, 249–250, 252–253, 254–255, 258–263, 265, 267–268, 271–272, 274–275, 277–278, 281–282
1956	81	*CW* 18:101 [On the Discourses of Buddha]

Jung's Writings on God (continued)

Year	Age	Work
1957	82	*Letters*: vol. 2, pp. 300–301, 302, 304–305, 311, 312–316, 327 *Letters*: vol. 2, pp. 342–343, 366, 368, 369, 371–372, 376–379, 380, 383–384, 394–396, 396 *C. G. Jung Speaking* [The Houston Films]
1958	83	*CW* 10:14 [The Undiscovered Self (Present and Future)] *CW* 10:16 [A Psychological View of Conscience] *CW* 10:15 [Flying Saucers] *CW* 10:17 [Good and Evil in Analytical Psychology] *CW* 18:48 [An Astrological Experiment] *CW* 18:103 [Jung and Religious Belief] *C. G. Jung Speaking* [A Talk with Students at the Institute] *C. G. Jung Speaking* [At the Basel Psychology Club]
1959	84	*Letters*: vol. 2, pp. 412, 422, 424, 434–436, 456, 468, 473 *Letters*: vol. 2, pp. 478, 483–484, 494–496, 511–512, 519, 522–523, 524, 525–526, 526–527 *C. G. Jung Speaking* [Talks with Miguel Serrano] *C. G. Jung Speaking* [On the Frontiers of Knowledge]

Jung's Writings on God (continued)

Year	Age	Work
1960	85	*C. G. Jung Speaking* [The "Face to Face" Interview] *C. G. Jung Speaking* [The Art of Living] *C. G. Jung Speaking* [An Eighty-Fifth Birthday Interview] *Letters:* vol. 2, pp. 541–542, 545, 556–557, 570–572, 584
1960–61?		*Memories, Dreams, Reflections:* On Life After Death *Memories, Dreams, Reflections:* Late Thoughts *Memories, Dreams, Reflections:* Epilogue
1961	86	*CW* 18:2 [Symbols and the Interpretation of Dreams] *Letters:* vol. 2, pp. 623, 624

How impressive is the great number of references to God in Jung's writings —more than 6000! Among Jung's individual writings and contacts with him by others who reported his remarks, which total more than 1530, the number of titles that mention God, God-image, Yahweh, and other designations of the Deity amount to more than 270. Thus, it can be seen that his preoccupation with the importance of the divine in his life and in the lives of others was very significant.

As seen above in this chronological listing of Jung's writings, lectures, interviews, and comments during encounters with other writers that contain references to

God, the greatest number appeared from 1930 onward, after he had reached 55 years of age. One must recognize, of course, that the time of publication of any work represents, in many cases, many years of work. As an example, his final great work, *Mysterium Coniunctionis*, whose subtitle was *An Inquiry into the Separation and Synthesis of Psychic Opposites in Alchemy*, was a work in progress from 1941 to 1954; he finished it in his 80th year. His interest in alchemy as being of significance in depth psychology was awakened in 1929, and engaged him again in the mid-1930s with his research and lectures on individual dream symbolism in relation to alchemy, and on religious ideas in alchemy, to be followed by further investigations during the 1940s (including relationships to psychotherapeutic problems, as in his work on the psychology of the transference) and his work on the relationship between philosophical alchemy and Christianity, which appeared in 1951 in *Aion: Researches into the Phenomenology of the Self.*

Such attention to the subject of psychic opposites, including contradictory aspects in the unconscious of a person, whose unifying principle of the self occupies a central position, and is the psychological carrier of the God-image in an individual, helps to explain the extensive use of "God" in Jung's work, particularly in his later years.

If a graph were constructed of the "occurrence of God" in Jung's reflections during his lifetime, it would consist of a few highlights until age 45—including remembrances from his childhood and youth in a Swiss Reformed pastor's home, clinical researches as a young psychiatrist in Zurich's mental sanitorium, and the professional activities that eventually separated him from being Freud's "heir" to becoming his own self through publication in

1911 of his work on transformation and symbols of the libido (published as *Psychology of the Unconscious* in English in 1916, later as *Symbols of Transformation*). International recognition came with his publication (in 1923) of *Psychological Types*, with more than 220 references to God.

From middle-age to old-age at 65 in 1940, Jung was engaged in a series of seminars in English, beginning with lectures given in the summer of 1923 in Cornwall, England, on human relationships in relation to the process of individuation, followed two years later in the summer at Swanage in Dorsetshire by a series on dreams and symbolism, with nearly 100 people attending. Those seminar lectures were not published.

The first of the long seminars in English (at Zurich) was given in 1925 on analytical psychology (with about 20 references to God). From 1928 to 1930, a longer seminar (51 meetings) was held on the subject of dream analysis with 54 recorded as members (with more than 100 references to God). This was followed shortly by a seminar on the interpretation of visions, meeting from October 1930 to March 1934 (with vacations), where more than 250 references to God were recorded. The longest seminar, which dealt with a psychological analysis of Nietzsche's *Zarathustra*, was held from May 1934 to February 1939 (with several long interruptions), with as many as 80 persons attending the more than 80 sessions, where more than 1000 references to God were recorded.

In total, then, nearly one-fourth of Jung's uses of the word God in writings and lectures occurred during seminars. It seems striking, therefore, to realize how much attention to "God" was given in groups of professional colleagues. Striking, also, was the less formal and more conversational manner of presenting ideas and concepts, along with the active participation by the members of the seminar.

Within this period of Jung's life (from age 45 to 65), his writings on religion and psychology, which included his study on religious ideas in alchemy (more than 150 references to God), mentioned above, as well as his 1937 lectures at Yale on psychology and religion (more than 100 references), and lectures in 1940 on a psychological approach to the dogma of the Trinity (more than 250 references) and in 1941 on transformation symbolism in the mass (nearly 100 references).

In later years, Jung still gave considerable attention to the relationship of psychology to religion, which culminated in 1951 with publications of his *Aion* (more than 350 references to God) and *Mysterium Coniunctionis* in 1955–1956 (more than 400 references). In the midst of those monumental works appeared his *Answer to Job* in 1952 (more than 600 references to God and Yahweh).

Jung had been occupied for years with the central problem in the Book of Job, which resulted in his very critical discussion of the Old Testament Yahweh of Job, and of the Christian appropriation of that God-concept. Even though, as he explained later, many different sources had nourished the stream of thoughts on the matter, the time to write about them came upon him suddenly and unexpectedly during a feverish illness. He explained that he could not write in a "coolly objective manner," but had to allow some "emotional subjectivity," to speak about certain books of the Bible. He agreed with the view of

Clement that monotheism clearly unites opposites in one God.

Among Jung's activities during the last twenty years of his life was his writing of letters, which, from the point of view of our subject of "God," was usually done in response to questions. Among more than 900 that had been selected from some 1600 letters, approximately one in six contained references to God. The major part of these occurred after publication of his *Answer to Job*. All of them provide valuable insight into his writing in a more informal style than in his books.

In a similar vein, Jung answered questions in 1957 from H. L. Philp, a British psychologist and theologian, and from David Cox, a British theologian, which were published by Philp in his book, *Jung and the Problem of Evil*, and were reprinted in volume 18 of Jung's *Collected Works*. "God" appeared in Jung's remarks 130 times.

In sum, it is remarkable how many times Jung "talked" about God in his concern for psychological understanding of the relationship between psychology and religion, in which he attempted to separate theology.

BIBLIOGRAPHY

The Collected Works of C. G. Jung (Princeton University)
[All volumes are listed here, though volumes 1 and 2 do not contain references to God, and volumes 3, 4, and 15 are not represented in this work.]

CW 1. *Psychiatric Studies* (1957; edn. 2, 1970).

CW 2. *Experimental Researches* (1973).

CW 3. *The Psychogenesis of Mental Disease* (1960).

CW 4. *Freud and Psychoanalysis* (1961).

CW 5. *Symbols of Transformation* (1956; edn. 2, 1974).

CW 6. *Psychological Types* (1971).

CW 7. *Two Essays on Analytical Psychology* (1953; edn. 2, 1972).

CW 8. *The Structure and Dynamics of the Psyche* (1960; edn. 2, 1969).

CW 9, i. *The Archetypes of the Collective Unconscious* (1959; edn. 2, 1968).

CW 9, ii. *Aion: Researches into the Phenomenology of the Self* (1959; edn.2, 1968).

CW 10. *Civilization in Transition* (1964; edn. 2, 1970).

CW 11. *Psychology of Religion: West and East* (1958; edn. 2, 1969).

CW 12. *Psychology and Alchemy* (1953; edn. 2, 1968).

CW 13. *Alchemical Studies* (1967).

CW 14. *Mysterium Coniunctionis: An Inquiry into the Separation and Synthesis of Psychic Opposites in Alchemy* (1963; edn. 2, 1970).

CW 15. *The Spirit in Man, Art, and Literature* (1966).

CW 16. *The Practice of Psychotherapy* (1954; edn. 2, 1966).

CW 17. *The Development of the Personality* (1954).

CW 18. *The Symbolic Life; Miscellaneous Writings* (1976).

CW 19. *General Bibliography of C. G. Jung's Writings* (1979; rev. ed., 1992).

CW 20. *General Index of the Collected Works of C. G. Jung* (1979).

CW A. *The Zofingia Lectures* (1983).

CW B. *Psychology of the Unconscious* (1992).

Campbell, Joseph, editor. *The Mysteries: Papers from the Eranos Yearbooks*, vol. 2. Princeton: Princeton University Press, 1955.

———. *Spirit and Nature: Papers from the Eranos Yearbooks*, vol. 1). Princeton: Princeton University Press, 1954.

Evans-Wentz, W. Y., editor. *The Tibetan Book of the Great Liberation*. London and New York: Oxford University Press, 1954.

Jung, C. G. *Analytical Psychology: Its Theory and Practice. The Travistock Lectures.* London: Routledge & Kegan Paul, 1968, 1976 paperback; New York: Pantheon Books/Random House, 1968; New York: Vintage Books/Random House, 1970 paperback; London: Ark Publications, 1986 paperback.

————. *Analytical Psychology: Notes of the Seminar Given in 1925 by C. G. Jung.* Princeton: Princeton University Press, 1986.

————. *Answer to Job.* London: Routledge & Kegan Paul, 1954; 1979 paperback; Great Neck, NY: Pastoral Psychology Book Club, 1956; Cleveland: Meridian Books, 1960 paperback; London: Hodder & Stoughton, 1965 paperback; Princeton: Princeton University Press, 1973 paperback; London: Ark Paperbacks, 1984.

————. *C. G. Jung Speaking: Interviews & Encounters.* William McGuire, ed., R. F. C. Hull and Ralph Manheim, trs. Princeton: Princeton University Press, 1977.

————. *Contributions to Analytical Psychology.* London: Kegan Paul, Trench, Trubner, 1928; New York: Harcourt, Brace, 1928.

————. *Dream Analysis: Notes of the Seminar Given in 1925 by C. G. Jung.* Princeton: Princeton University, n.d.

————. *A Critical Dictionary of Jungian Analysis.* Edited by Andrew Samuels, Bani Shorter, and Fred Plaut. London & New York: Routledge & Kegan Paul, 1986 paperback.

————. *The Integration of the Personality.* New York & Toronto: Farrar & Rinehart, 1939; London: Kegan Paul, 1940.

————. *Letters* (2 volumes). London: Routledge & Kegan Paul, 1973–1976; Princeton: Princeton University Press, 1973–1976.

———. *Man and His Symbols.* New York: Doubleday, 1964; London: Aldus Books, 1964, 1975 paperback; New York: Dell, 1968 paperback.

———. *Memories, Dreams, Reflections.* London: Collins with Routledge & Kegan Paul, 1962; New York: Pantheon, 1963 paperback, rev. 1973; New York: Vintage/Random House, 1965 paperback, rev. 1989; London: Collins, 1967 paperback; London: Flamingo Fontana, 1983 paperback.

———. *Modern Man in Search of a Soul.* London: Kegan Paul, Trench, Trubner, 1933; Toronto: McLeod, 1933; New York: Harcourt, Brace, 1933; New York: Harvest Books/Harcourt, Brace, Jovanovich, 1955 paperback; London: Routledge & Kegan Paul, 1970 paperback; London: Ark Publications, 1984 paperback.

———. *Nietzsche's Zarathustra: Notes of the Seminar Given in 1934–1939 by C. G. Jung* (2 volumes). Princeton: Princeton University Press, 1938; New Haven: Yale Paperback, 1960.

———. *Psychology and Religion.* New Haven: Yale University Press; London: Oxford University Press, 1938; New Haven: Yale Paperback, 1960.

———. *The Spirit Mercury.* New York: Analytical Psychology Club, 1953 printing for private circulation.

———. *The Undiscovered Self.* London: Routledge & Kegan Paul, 1958, 1984 paperback; New York: New American Library, 1959, 1974 paperback.

———. *Visions: Notes of the Seminar Given in 1930–1934 by C. G. Jung* (2 volumes). Zurich: Spring Publications, 1976 paperback; Princeton: Princeton University Press, 1997.

Philp, Howard L. *Jung and the Problem of Evil.* London: Rockliff, 1958; New York: Robert M. McBride, 1959.

Samuels, Andrew, Bani Shorter, and Fred Plaut, editors. *A Critical Dictionary of Jungian Analysis.* London and New York: Routledge & Kegan Paul, 1986.

White, Victor. *God and the Unconscious.* London: Harvill Press, 1952.

Wilhelm, Richard, translator. *The Secret of the Golden Flower.* New York: Harcourt, Brace, 1931.

Yungblut, John R. *Discovering God Within.* Philadelphia: Westminster Press, 1979.

———. *Rediscovering the Christ.* New York: Seabury Press, 1974.

———. *Rediscovering Prayer.* New York, Seabury Press, 1972.

INDEX

Donald R. Dyer was born in the mountains of Colorado in 1918, was married in 1942, and has two daughters and one granddaughter. He received his B.A. at Stanford University (1947), M.S. (1948) and Ph.D. (1950) at Northwestern University, and was a professor at the University of Florida/Gainesville from 1950–1962, which included a two–year Fulbright lectureship at Universidad de San Marcos in Peru. He was a Geographic Attaché in the U.S. Foreign Service in Rio de Janeiro, Mexico City, and New Delhi. Based in the Bureau of Intelligence and Research in the State Department as a map and publications procurement officer from 1968–1978, he carried out missions to more than 80 countries. In 1971 he joined Friends (Quakers) and was convinced by Quaker writer and lecturer John R. Yungblut of the value of the famous Swiss psychiatrist C. G. Jung's depth psychology, and of Teilhard de Chardin's "continuing creation." He retired in 1979 and devotes his time to gardening and Jungian studies, becoming a founding member and president of C. G. Jung Society of the Triangle Area. He has conducted workshops on Jungian themes, participated in study-group courses, and attended various Jungian conferences. He has written *Cross-Currents of Jungian Thought: An Annotated Bibliography* and his book in progress is *George Fox* (founder of Quakerism) *and The Inner Light: A Jungian Interpretation.* He lives in Chapel Hill, NC.